LNER A3 Pacific No. 4472 *Flying Scotsman* prepares to depart from King's Cross to York on July 4 1999 following a three-year overhaul. **ROBIN JONES**

World steam records: a Great British success

In the Thirties, Britain – like many other western nations – reeled under the effects of the Great Depression, with mass unemployment... especially in Scotland and the north of England.

Yet out of the gloom and despondency, the people of these islands proved that we could still take on the whole world... and win.

It was on the 1-in-200 Stoke Bank, a seemingly unremarkable and very rural section of main line railway in Lincolnshire, that world steam locomotive speed records would come tumbling.

First there was *Flying Scotsman*, which in 1934 became the first steam locomotive in the world to officially reach 100mph. Then sister locomotive *Papyrus* set a new record of 108mph.

It was followed soon afterwards by streamlined A4 Pacific No. 2509 *Silver Link*, which managed a speed of 112.5mph.

Finally, there was No. 4468 *Mallard*, which set an all-time world steam locomotive speed record of 126mph.

The man behind these legendary feats which emphasised the Great in Britain was London & North Eastern Railway chief mechanical engineer Sir Nigel Gresley. He designed these and many other groundbreaking locomotives which were superior to everything that had gone before.

The economic morass at the begining of the decade could so easily have led to a situation where everyone might have given up hope.

Yet it was still a great age of competition, one in which the LNER, as the operator of the East Coast Main Line between London King's Cross and Edinburgh, wanted to show that it could link England to Scotland faster that the London, Midland & Scottish Railway's West Coast Main Line alternative from St Pancras to Glasgow, and the splendid Pacific locomotives designed by Gresley's great rival, Sir William Stanier.

The net result was the golden age of rail travel, in which luxury named trains such as the 'Coronation' and the 'Elizabethan' blazed a trail towards what should have been a bright new future, had the Second World War not intervened.

Gresley has been feted as the greatest British locomotive engineer of all time. Yet it was ordinary British footplate crews, drivers and firemen, who took his machines towards their limits – and beyond – in classic feats of derring-do and endurance.

Those behind the controls of a record-breaking locomotives would be feted as heroes by the national press when they returned to King's Cross. They were the superstars, the pop idols, of their generation. However, the next day they would be back in their overalls on their next turns of duty, likely to be on run-of-the-mill scheduled services where superlatives were not necessarily required.

As Britain beamed with pride at such achievements, other nations looked on with awe and envy.

This volume is the story not only of those famous locomotives which became household words, but of the route from London to Edinburgh – from Roman times onwards – and how human endeavour, innovation and excellence shortened the journey times between these two capital cities.

There was the Great North Road and its rival stagecoach operators, which went out of business when three railway companies eventually joined up to create one great 393 mile through route, and almost immediately looked at the issue of speed.

The steam age did not give up without a fight: in 1959 A4 Pacific *Sir Nigel Gresley*, named after the genius designer, recorded a new post-war steam record of 112mph – where else but on Stoke Bank.

The diesel era not only produced some of the finest examples of modern traction in the form of the English Electric Deltics, but also saw more records broken with the introduction of the hugely-successful InterCity Class 125 High Speed Trains.

Finally, the electrification of the whole route led to a Class 91 locomotive officially being declared the fastest in Britain.

The East Coast Main Line is taken for granted by the untold tens of thousands of commuters and travellers who use it on a daily basis.

Yet it is a great monument, not only to those who built it – in the days when picks and shovels not JCBs and earthmovers were used to dig cuttings and create massive embankments by hand – but to many generations of railwaymen who showed on a daily basis that they wanted their line to be the best.

Gresley's art deco streamlined A4 Pacifics remain a definitive icon of everything that was brilliant about Britain – a nation of innovation and determination which could so easily lead the world again.

Robin Jones
October 2011

Contents

AUTHOR
Robin Jones

SUB EDITORS
Karen Veasey, Tim Hartley

DESIGN
Leanne Lawrence
Charlotte Pearson

PRODUCTION MANAGER
Craig Lamb

PUBLISHER
Dan Savage

COMMERCIAL DIRECTOR
Nigel Hole

**BUSINESS DEVELOPMENT
DIRECTOR**
Terry Clark

MANAGING DIRECTOR
Brian Hill

PUBLISHED BY
Mortons Media Group Ltd,
Media Centre, Morton Way,
Horncastle, Lincs LN9 6JR
Tel: 01507 523456

PRINTED BY
William Gibbons and Sons,
Wolverhampton

ISBN
978-1-906167-71-4

FROM THE PUBLISHERS OF
**HERITAGE
RAILWAY**

Mortons Media Group Ltd. All rights reserved. No part of this
publication may be reproduced or transmitted in any form or
by any means, electronic or mechanical, including
photocopying, recording, or any information storage retrieval
system without prior permission in writing from the publisher

Cover: LNER A4 Pacific No. 60007 *Sir Nigel Gresley* storms across Greatford level crossing north of Peterborough as it heads up Stoke Bank with a charter train in December 2009. **ROBIN JONES**

Main picture: A classic line-up of East Coast Main Line motive power at the north end of York station on March 19, 1978. From left to right are Stirling Single No. 1, North Eastern Railway 4-4-0 1621, Ivatt Atlantic No. 251, world steam record holder No. 4468 *Mallard*, Deltic No. 55013 *The Black Watch* and High Speed Train No. 254009. **GAVIN MORRISON**

254 009

CHAPTER ONE

London to Edinburgh
In 45½ hours

It is known that the Romans used basic railways in their mines, but even their advanced technology didn't bring them anywhere near to thinking about building a line 393 miles long to link London and Edinburgh.

The Romans were, however, expert road builders, and laid the foundations – literally - of much that became the Great North Road, the fastest land means of linking the two capital cities for the best part of two millennia. That is, until the invention of the steam locomotive.

We do not know what name the Romans gave to it, but the road we call Ermine Street was the great highway built from Londinium to Lindum Colonia (Lincoln) and Eboracum (York). The Old English name was Earninga Straete, named after a tribe called the Earningas, who lived in southern Cambridgeshire and parts of Hertfordshire. It is also known as the Old North Road.

The Romans built great durable highways firstly for military purposes, to subdue the country they began conquering in AD44, and then for trade and administrative use. North of York, the former use was of paramount importance, serving the great frontier of the Roman Empire, Hadrian's Wall, which stretched from the Solway First to the mouth of the River Tyne.

The Romans were, for a brief time at least, not content with the wall built to keep out the Picts from the north penning the legions in too, and set about expanding their empire even further north. In AD142, the Emperor Antoninus Pius ordered the construction of a much more basic structure, the stone and turf Antonine Wall, stretching from the Clyde to the Forth. It has 16 forts and numerous smaller fortlets between them.

A rare section of single-carriageway A1 in Scotland just across the border.
STEVE KEIRETSU/CREATIVE COMMONS

The Romans struggled to subdue southernmost Scotland, and gave up after 20 years, abandoning the northernmost wall. The Emperor Septimius Severus had another go at occupying the Antonine Wall in AD 208 but the occupation lasted only a few years before another retreat, abandoning the structure forever. Incidentally, it is today bisected by the Bo'ness & Kinneil Railway, which is operated by the Scottish Railway Preservation Society.

To serve the wall, the Romans built roads, extending northwards the British pattern of north-south routes that ran either side of England's central spine, the Pennine chain.

We do not know exactly where the Roman roads in Scotland ran, but it is likely there were three: the westernmost near Carlisle, following roughly today's A74, one on the other side of the mountains near the modern-day A68, and maybe a third, which crosses the River Tweed at Tweedmouth, near the future Berwick-on-Tweed. They were natural routes indeed to follow: it is generally forgotten that a reasonable network of primitive roads existed in Britain before the Romans arrived to improve them; the Great North Road is said to have been trod by Phoenician traders as well as ancient Britons.

At one point, on Stoke Bank in Lincolnshire, the section of Ermine Street also known as High Dyke, and now designated as the B6403, is crossed by the East Coast Main Line. However, much, much more on Stoke Bank later.

The Romans left Britain in 410AD, and when they retreated, so did their road-building technology. Mankind's progress went backwards somewhat in this respect. The Roman road remained in place for centuries, but were not repaired, and many became overgrown or lost.

The A1 today bypasses Stamford, a former bustling coaching town. **ROBIN JONES**

This advertisement etched into the stonework of this Stamford building dates from its days as one of the most prosperous coaching towns in England. **ROBIN JONES**

THE GREAT NORTH ROAD

By the 12th century, flooding and damage by traffic to the Old North Road led to the establishment of an alternative route out of London via Muswell Hill. It became part of the Great North Road, the premier highway that linked London to York and then Edinburgh, with a total length of 409 miles.

For centuries, most principal roads in the British Isles were little more than muddy paths, full of potholes and almost as much an obstacle as an aid to horses and carts.

Tudor statutes placed responsibility on each parish to maintain all its roads, but while this alleviated the situation on a local basis, it was no use for the long-distance routes used by travellers and waggoners.

Matters came to a head in London in the 17th century, when the capital's trade increased to the point where the amount of carts going in and out of the city caused such damage to the roads that the parish

workforces could never keep up. It became clear that with limited finance and resources available, the best way forward was to select a single highway into the city as a main artery and raise money from passing travellers to finance the upkeep of its surfaces.

In 1663, an Act of Parliament awarded local magistrates powers to install tollgates on a section of the Great North Road. So the stretch between Wadesmill in Hertfordshire and Stilton in Huntingdonshire, became one of Britain's first toll roads.

During the first 30 years of the 18th century, many stretches of main roads leading into London became controlled by turnpike trusts. It was a popular and pragmatic solution, even though travellers many did their best to avoid paying their tolls at the toll houses. Trusts could demand extra fees from users during the summer to pay for watering the road in order to lay the dust thrown up by fast-moving vehicles. A

The Bell at Stilton is one of the ancient coaching inns on the Great North Road. Thanks to the coaching trade, the village evolved as a trading post between London and Edinburgh for many commodities and the inn's landlord Cooper Thornhill first sold the local cheese from the premises, not only to passing travellers but also into London. **ROBIN JONES**

turnpike road, New North Road and Canonbury Road (now the A1200) was built in 1812. It linked the start of the Old North Road in Shoreditch with the Great North Road at Highbury Corner.

The term turnpike derives from the similarity of the toll gates to barriers once used to defend against attack by cavalry, where a row of sharpened pikes was attached to horizontal members and fixed at one end to an upright pole or axle, which could be rotated to open or close a gate.

By 1825, around 1,000 turnpike trusts controlled 18,000 miles of road in England and Wales. Before the turnpike trusts, in terms of long-distance travellers who needed to travel at speed, roads were sufficient only to accommodate riders on horseback. The better surfaces improved communication links, and laid the way for the stagecoach era.

The Great North Road became a primary route used by mail coaches between London, York and Edinburgh. The traditional starting point of the Great North Road, from where mileages were once measured, was the former Hicks Hall at London's Smithfield, but with the building of the General Post Office in 1829, stagecoaches switched to the modern route subsequently classified as the A1, following Aldersgate Street and Goswell Road before joining the old route at the Angel, a key staging post.

With the building of the General Post Office at St Martin's-le-Grand in London in 1829, mail coaches started using an alternative to the Great North Road, one used by the modern A1, beginning at the GPO building and following Aldersgate Street, pictured at Barbican station. **ROBIN JONES**

Today the bypassed Great North Road through Stilton hosts the annual cheese rolling festival each May, although wooden blocks are substituted for the real thing. **ROBIN JONES**

This classic 1934 LNER poster compares the record flight on horseback wrongly attributed to Dick Turpin and his trusty steed Black Bess with the speed of its express trains. **NRM**

THE STAGECOACH ERA

The earliest record of coach travel from London to the coaching 'capital' of Stamford was in 1685, when the fare for a two-day journey from the George Inn at Aldersgate was a pound. If you wanted to travel to York, it was another two days.

The improvement of major roads through turnpike trusts cut the travelling time between London and Stamford to just a day by 1770, and the fare was also cut, to 16 shillings. By then, a journey up the Great North Road from the capital to Edinburgh would take at least four days.

Royal Mail coaches made their debut on the road in the 1780s and by 1792, the 'Original Stamford Fly' stagecoach service linked the town to London offering a travelling time of just 16 hours.

The towns that were fortunate to lie alongside the Great North Road developed like pearls on a necklace, as the increasing through traffic brought prosperity in its wake. The first staging posts going northwards were Highgate, Barnet, Hatfield, Baldock, Biggleswade and Alconbury.

It must be remembered that despite the collection of tolls from road users to finance the upkeep, this major route was still in a very parlous state, with coaches frequently overturning in gaping potholes, and speeds being limited to 6-8mph at best.

The Great North Road still leads past the George Hotel into Stamford, described as the finest stone town in England. **ROBIN JONES**

LNER A1 Pacific No. 2579 *Dick Turpin*, pictured at King's Cross in 1934, recalls the legendary highwayman of the Great North Road. It is about to depart northward with the 'Flying Scotsman'. **STEVE ARMITAGE COLLECTION**

In Georgian times, coaching towns like Stamford were the equivalent of a modern-day motorway service station. To cater for stagecoach traffic, with frequent overnight stops for travellers and the essential changes of horses, existing hostelries had to be enlarged and new inns opened, while the town's shopkeepers did a roaring trade. Many of the great coaching inns on the Great North Road survive to this day, such as the Bell Inn at Stilton – where Stilton cheese was first served – and the George Hotel in Stamford. The novelist Sir Walter Scott said that the view up to St Mary's church in Stamford was the finest sight on the road between London and Edinburgh.

The stagecoach route led from Stamford to Colsterworth, Grantham, Newark, Retford and Bawtry to Doncaster, Selby and York. The first recorded stage coach operation to York was in 1658.

While York was the first terminus of the stagecoach route from London, a new route running from Doncaster to Ferrybridge, Wetherby, Boroughbridge, Northallerton and Darlington provided a more direct way to Edinburgh, the ultimate destination.

Faster mail coaches began using the new route in 1786, and competition led to rivals speeding up their services.

The years 1815-35 were the golden age of coaching and brought the travelling time from London to York down to 20 hours and from London to Edinburgh to 45 1/2 hours. Cutting-edge technology indeed: Hadrian and Antonius would have been impressed.

For four centuries, attempts have been made to use cutting-edge transport technology to reduce journey times between London and Edinburgh, the Scots capital dominated by its castle. **ROBIN JONES**

STAND AND DELIVER

The reputation of the Great North Road was not always linked with the benefits of speedy travel between the two capital cities, and had many darker moments.

The road, especially its most deserted sections, was long the haunt of highwaymen and footpads, who would famously relieve rich travellers of their wealth with the cry "your money or your life!"

The most notorious highwayman of all in these parts was John 'Swift Nick' Nevison, whose six-man gang had the Talbot Inn at Newark-on-Trent as their headquarters and would rob travellers on the Great North Road as far north as York and as far south as Huntingdon.

The son of a wool merchant, Nevison was given his nickname by none other than Charles II, who displayed a sneaking admiration for the rascal, if only because of his marathon ride on horseback from London to York.

In *A Tour Through the Whole Island of Great Britain*, Daniel Defoe recorded that Nevison robbed a traveller at Gads Hill in Kent one summer morning in 1676, ironically at the same spot near Rochester where Shakespeare's Falstaff committed a similar though fictitious felony in *Henry IV Part One*.

Nevison then galloped away on a bay mare, crossed the Thames on a ferry and rode at an unearthly speed to York, resting his horse only for short periods on the way.

After riding for more than 200 miles, he arrived at York, changed his clothes and spruced himself up, and then attended a bowling green where he knew the Lord Mayor of York would be playing. He spoke to the mayor and

> THE ROAD, ESPECIALLY ITS MOST DESERTED SECTIONS, WAS LONG THE HAUNT OF HIGHWAYMEN AND FOOTPADS, WHO WOULD FAMOUSLY RELIEVE RICH TRAVELLERS OF THEIR WEALTH WITH THE CRY "YOUR MONEY OR YOUR LIFE!"

laid a bet on the outcome of the game – ensuring that the time he placed the bet, 8pm, was remembered.

Nevison was subsequently arrested for the Gads Hill robbery – but to everyone's astonishment, produced the mayor as an alibi. The court refused to believe that a man who had committed a crime in Kent could have been in York at 8pm the same day.

Nevison was not only cleared but emerged as a folk hero, impressing even the king. It was said that he never used violence in any of his robberies. Nevertheless, he was arrested on several occasions, once escaping from Wakefield prison, and on another occasion being sentenced to transportation to Tangiers, only to escape before the ship sailed from Tilbury. He even managed to get an accomplice to pose as a doctor and pronounce him dead of the plague to escape the strong arm of the law once again.

His end came after he killed a constable called Fletcher who tried to arrest him, and was caught by bounty hunters at an inn at Sandal near Wakefield.

At the age of 45 he was hanged at York Castle on May 4, 1684 and buried in an unmarked grave.

After his death, Nevison himself was robbed – of the reputation of his greatest feat, for a subsequent writer credited his marathon ride from Kent to York to an even more famous highwayman of the Great North Road, none other than Dick Turpin, and his horse Black Bess, and so the story was cast in legend, but attributed to the wrong man, who had lived half a century before.

The Great North Road at Highgate as seen before the coming of the turnpike, with its muddy rutted surface.

A Great North Road pub sign illustration of a typical stagecoach, in the era when rival operators began cutting journey times from London to Edinburgh, with no steam trains yet in sight. **ROBIN JONES**

FROM STAGECOACHES TO CARS

The zenith of the coaching trade was around 1830, when Stamford boasted 40 mail coaches and 30 passenger carrying services passing through each day, not to mention numerous carriers of freight.

A quarter of a century before, few of the landlords doing a roaring trade along the Great North Road would have given a damn if they had even heard about a Cornish mining engineer called Richard Trevithick demonstrating in public, for the first time, a steam railway locomotive, on the Penydarren Tramroad near Merthyr Tydfil. However, they were given just cause to quake in their boots with the successful opening on September 15, 1830 of the Liverpool & Manchester Railway, the world's first inter-city passenger line, in which all the trains were hauled for most of the distance solely by steam locomotives.

The great period of railway building that followed consigned the stagecoaches to history. Not only could they not compete in terms of speed, but the great coaching towns, particularly if they were bypassed by railways as happened in the case of Stamford, lost their livelihoods almost overnight.

The last coach from London to Newcastle left in 1842 and the last from Newcastle to Edinburgh in July 1847. The days of the highwayman were numbered too: the last mounted robbery in England was said to have taken place in 1831.

The Great North Road outlived the stagecoach era, and in the early 20th century, saw its first motor cars.

In 1921, when the ministry of Transport began numbering roads, it was designated the A1, the first and foremost in Britain.

Just as it became a key arterial route for the horse-drawn mail coaches, in the 20th century it became a primary route for motor traffic competing against the railways.

It became so busy that by 1927, its first town passes were built, around Barnet and Hatfield. Chester-le-Street, Durham and Ferryhill followed in the 1930s, and in 1960, Stamford the great coaching town and Durham were also bypassed. Retford followed in 1961 and St Neots in 1971, as parts of the route were widened to motorway status as the A1(M), much of the rest being dual carriageway. The Hatfield tunnel was opened in 1986.

The A1 is deemed to start from St Paul's Cathedral and finish at the eastern end of Princes Street near Edinburgh Waverley station where the A7, A8 and A900 roads meet.

Scotch Corner in North Yorkshire, marks the point where traffic bound for Glasgow parts from that heading for Edinburgh.

The Great North Road had, for centuries, established both the government and public desire for speedy travel between the two capitals, and when the stagecoaches were superseded by the railway, it was left to the steam locomotive to take up the baton where they had left off.

In doing so, the route would be elevated on to the world stage, immortalising the Britain of the 1930s as the world leader in terms of land transport technology.

The Great North Road is characterised by its generous width and sweeping verges as it passed through towns and villages like Long Bennington in Lincolnshire. **ROBIN JONES**

One other, and often overlooked claim to fame of the Great North Road in terms of speed, is that Goswell Road, one of the early stretches in London, is held by some to be the starting point for the first successful four-minute mile run, by James Parrott on May 9, 1770. He is said to have run down Old Street before finishing at St Leonard's in Shoreditch.

The sporting authorities of the time accepted the claim as genuine, having the benefit of the invention of John Harrison's chronometer by then. Such a device was said to have measured the four minutes correctly, but the record is not recognised by modern sporting bodies, and so generations of schoolboys are now told that the world's first four-minute mile was run on May 6, 1954 by Roger Bannister, nearly 184 years after Parrott. ■

The end of the A1 in Edinburgh.
KLAUS/CREATIVE COMMONS

CHAPTER TWO

First over the border

The East Coast Main Line broadly parallels the route of the A1. Linking London with Yorkshire, the North East and Scotland, it is one of Britain's key trunk routes. As with most other British trunk routes from the great age of railway building, it was not designed and built by one company, but came into being piecemeal fashion.

Three companies, the North British, North Eastern and Great Northern railways built sections of the line to serve their own needs, but mindful that one day they would link up to provide a fast route between the two capital cities that would become a backbone of post-Industrial Revolution Britain.

It is easy to assume that the starting point for construction would be London, with the route extending further northwards into the provinces as more capital was raised. However, it was the North British Railway that built the first section, completing its line from Edinburgh to Berwick-upon-Tweed in 1846, and in doing so became the first railway to cross the border into England.

The Great Northern Railway completed its line from King's Cross to Shaftholme, a tiny village north of Doncaster, in 1850.

Finally, the North Eastern Railway came together through a series of amalgamations and in 1871 built the final section needed to provide a direct through route.

EDINBURGH'S FIRST STEAM RAILWAY

After several early schemes came to nothing, the Edinburgh & Glasgow Railway was formed in 1835 and on July 4, 1838 received Parliamentary powers to build Scotland's first inter-city line. The first passenger services between Edinburgh Haymarket and Glasgow Queen Street ran on February 21, 1842 and goods traffic began that March.

One disadvantage was that Haymarket lay on the western edge of the capital, whereas Queen Street was in Glasgow's centre. Nonetheless, the railway was a huge success, carrying 1600 people a day during its first 10 months.

It soon became clear that a more convenient terminus was needed in Edinburgh city centre and in 1844 an eastward extension from Haymarket was planned. A new station, Edinburgh General, was opened on May 17, 1847.

CROSSING THE BORDER

Six weeks before the Edinburgh & Glasgow opened, its chairman, John Learmonth, held a meeting with a group of Edinburgh gentlemen, who were keen on building a railway running eastwards to the fishing port of Dunbar 30 miles away. They formed a provisional committee to promote the scheme, under the banner of the North British Railway.

Local investors did not believe that the scheme would reap sufficient dividends, and so the new company looked further afield, to the border country. It was decided to build a line all the way to Berwick-upon-Tweed, taking a railway across the border for the first time.

The scheme attracted sufficient investors, albeit they mainly came from south of the border.

At the time, stagecoach services ran along the Great North Road to Edinburgh and there were sailings between Leith and London, but while they made communication possible, it would never be as attractive as completing the journey by rail in a fraction of the time.

While the Edinburgh & Glasgow had struggled to win Parliamentary powers, the North British gained its Act on July 4, 1844 with little opposition, and work began almost immediately – not on the main line, but its first branch, the 4½ mile route from Longniddry to Haddington, an important market town that had been bypassed by the main line to cut down on expenditure of tackling the hilly terrain.

The terminus was also North Bridge, allowing through running from the Edinburgh & Glasgow.

The line from there to Berwick was built by 12 different contractors within two

LNER A4 Pacific No. 60007 *Sir Nigel Gresley* crosses the Royal Border Bridge at Berwick with a heritage era charter. **BRIAN SHARPE**

years. Money was saved by the engineers following contours around cliffs rather than tunnelling through spurs.

At Cocksburnpath, an 11ft high, six-span stone bridge took the line over the Dunglass burn, with large embankments either side. This part of the line caused problems, not only with waterlogging, but with the labour force. Near the summit, the topmost ridge was pierced by the 267-yard Penmanshiel Tunnel.

The navvies comprised Irish Catholics and Scottish protestants – cultural opponents to put it mildly. The men were paid in tokens to be redeemed only at the contractor's shop, where whisky was heavily promoted.

The local population came to dread pay day. In October 1844, matters came to a head when religion sparked a riot through the local area, bringing work on the railway to a standstill, and ill feeling between the warring parties lasted well over a year.

Not everyone welcomed the coming of the railway. One James Blackadder feared that God-fearing Scotland would be threatened by the heathen English influence channelled north by the line.

He took out press advertisements warning his fellow countrymen of the latest Sabbath desecration taking place in England – which took the form of the running of trains on a Sunday.

On August 3, 1975, LNER D49 4-4-0 No. 246 *Morayshire* and Caledonian Railway 0-4-4T No. 419 pass Dunbar with a rake of vintage coaches from the Scottish Railway Preservation Society's former base at Falkirk to Shildon for the Stockton & Darlington Railway 150th anniversary celebrations. **BRIAN SHARPE**

The original Berwick station as built by the North British Railway had a castellated appearance. **NETWORK RAIL**

Network Rail's plaque at Dunbar station marking 150 years of trains using the line between Edinburgh and Berwick. **ROBIN JONES**

THE YO-YO TOWN

Berwick station would never be passed by planning authorities in our heritage-conscious age... for its construction in 1847 required the demolition of the great hall of Berwick Castle.

The castle was founded in the 12th century by the Scottish king David I. A plaque in the main building today records that it was there on November 17, 1292 that John Balliol (also known as Baliol, or de Balliol) was proclaimed by 104 Scottish 'auditors' as the new King John of Scotland, a situation manipulated by the English king Edward I, in preference to the less amenable Robert Bruce, grandfather of Robert the Bruce.

However, Edward failed to show Balliol much respect, and after Scottish barons concluded a treaty with France that became known as the Auld Alliance, Balliol abdicated in July 1296 and became Edward's prisoner.

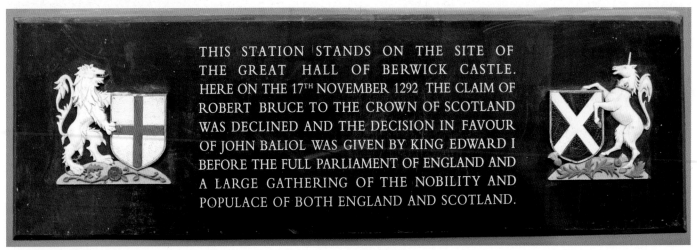

The plaque commemorating Berwick Castle's place in Scottish history. **ROBIN JONES**

Berwick-upon-Tweed station today: modern trains pass through the heart of what was once one of Britain's great castles. **ROBIN JONES**

Both Berwick and its castle changed hands more than 13 times during the English-Scottish conflicts between 1147 and 1482. The castle's position in the disputed border country made it one of the most important fortresses in England. New battlements were built to protect Berwick in the 16th century but as the nations became slightly more peaceful neighbours the castle faded in strategic importance, with large parts being used as a source of stone for other buildings, such as Berwick's parish church of Holy Trinity during the reign of Oliver Cromwell.

The spot where Edward took oaths of allegiance from Scottish nobility in 1296 is now covered by railway platforms.

In 1482, Berwick was captured by Richard Duke of Gloucester, the future Richard III, but it never was officially merged into England, which nonetheless has administered the town ever since. The situation led to the unique anomaly where it appears to be the 'county town' of Berwickshire... which is in another country.

The Act of Union of 1707 which saw England and Scotland joined ended the dispute, so Berwick remains within the laws and legal system of England and Wales. However, there are still calls for it to be returned to Scotland, and the town's football team, Berwick Rangers, play in the Scottish League rather than the English system, for geographical reasons.

The North British Railway had reached Berwick in 1846, and made do with a basic temporary station until the present one was built. Not all of the castle was lost: the former west wall of the castle still marks the boundary of the now-defunct goods yard.

The surviving west wall of Berwick Castle by the old goods yard. **ROBIN JONES**

THE FIRST TRAINS TO ENGLAND

Huge celebrations marked the North British Railway's first operations on June 18, 1846, when two new 0-4-2s hauled two maroon-liveried trains out of Edinburgh. On the day, two trains using a total of 50 out of the company's 146 carriages used nine engines to take the invited guests from Edinburgh to Berwick and back.

Regular services began four days later with five trains each way between Edinburgh and Berwick, from where there were stagecoach connections to Newcastle. A journey with only one stop, at Dunbar, took 90 minutes, while a stopping train took 2½ hours.

Dunbar station. The port had been the intended original destination of the North British Railway's first line. **ROBIN JONES**

The British Rail sign marking the point where the ECML crosses the border between England and Scotland. **CALLUM BLACK/CREATIVE COMMONS**

The standard of passenger accommodation was higher than on most railways of the day. First class vehicles were broadly based on stagecoach concept, with enclosed compartments, but enclosed carriages with windows were also provided for second-class travellers. Third class passengers not only had benches to sit on, but roofs to shelter beneath too, a direct contrast with the open seatless vehicles on the Edinburgh & Glasgow.

Hawthorn of Newcastle provided 26 double-framed 0-4-2s followed by six 2-2-2s and 15 2-4-0s, while freight, in form of Lothian coal traffic and borders agricultural produce, was handled by an increasing number of 0-6-0s hauled both the established Lothian coal flows and developing agricultural traffic from the Borders.

'The Elizabethan' bound for King's Cross departs from Edinburgh Waverley on July 25, 1953, powered by A4 Pacific No. 60004 *William Whitelaw*. **BRIAN MORRISON**

North British Railway J36 0-6-0 No. 673 *Maude* leaves Edinburgh Waverley with a railtour to Inverkeithing on May 4, 1980. The locomotive is now displayed in the National Railway Museum at York. **BRIAN SHARPE**

WHISKY BY NO MEANS GALORE

Today it comes as a surprise to many people to learn that until the 19th century, there were still customs controls in place between England and Scotland. The 1707 Act had not abolished the frontier with respect to 'colonial liquor' and similar restrictions applied as to when crossing the channel into France.

A month after the North British Railway opened, the company announced the first-ever excursion from Glasgow to England, with the two Scottish railways combining to lay on the trip for 400 passengers, stopping off at Edinburgh and Dunbar.

However, the trip turned sour when the train stopped at Berwick. Customs men pounced on the unsuspecting passengers and opened their baggage, seizing whisky where it was found.

The excursion was followed by regular arrests of both passengers and staff for smuggling whisky. The railway complained about the delays to its services caused by the revenue men while the customers officers complained that obstacles were being placed in their way.

Eventually, the situation ended when the law was changed to allow whisky to be carried across the border.

DESTROYED BY FLOODS

On August 30, the engine of a train carrying none other than North British Locomotive Superintendent Robert Thornton hit floodwater near Linton and the engine came off the track with the leading coach and plunged down an embankment. Nobody was killed.

It rained throughout the ensuing September and, to cut a long story short, there was little

hiding the fact that parts of the line had been built in a hurry and on the cheap when extensive flooding washed away sections of trackbed along with bridges and embankments along the coastal section. The result was that 19 miles of the route became rendered impassable.

The North British Railway had killed off the stagecoach services along its route overnight, and so any form of other horse-drawn transport that could be found at short notice, even ordinary carts, was pressed into service to connect the two operational halves of the line.

The damage highlighted the shoddy workmanship in much of the building of the line and its infrastructure, especially with regard the section of the cliffs north of Berwick.

The destruction was repaired in piecemeal fashion, and it was not until the end of the century that serious work was carried out to bring the railway fully up to standard.

Overnight on August 12, 1948, violent thunderstorms washed away part of the ECML in Berwickshire. This is the state of Free Kirk Bridge near Granthouse the following day. **NRM**

Robert Stephenson, the great railway engineer who designed the Royal Border Bridge for the York, Newcastle and Berwick Railway

The 9.50am express from Aberdeen arrives at Edinburgh Waverley on July 31, 1953 behind Class A2 Pacific No. 60629 *Pearl Diver,* which took over the train at Dundee. This was the only locomotive in the A2 fleet to have been rebuilt with a double blast pipe and multiple valve regulator. **BRIAN MORRISON**

A4 Pacific No. 60009 union of South Africa passes East Linton with a southbound railtour. **BRIAN SHARPE**

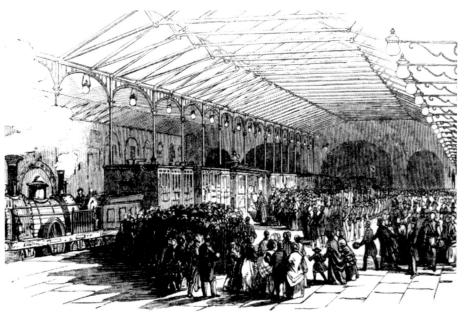

The arrival at Berwick of the Royal Train from London, carrying Queen Victoria to open the Royal Border Bridge. **ILLUSTRATED LONDON NEWS**

Locomotives being built in the North British Railway's locomotive works at Cowlairs on the western side of the Glasgow-Edinburgh main line at Carlisle Street in Glasgow prior to the Grouping of 1923. It was the first works in Britain to build locomotives, carriages and wagons in the same place. Locomotive building here ended when the LNER was formed, but the works carried on until 1968. **SRPS**

SOUTHERN CONNECTIONS

After the damaged line was reopened, North British directors were concerned that the Leith to London ships were still carrying twice as many passengers as the line.

However, there was no need for them to fret for too long, for within months the railway had been linked to the rapidly-expanding English network.

The Newcastle & Berwick Railway meanwhile reached the south bank of the River Tweed in March 1847, effectively linking Berwick to the Brandling Junction Railway at Gateshead.

However, it was another 18 months before a temporary viaduct across the river was built to allow through running between Edinburgh and Newcastle via the North British Railway.

The temporary bridge was superseded in July 1850 when Queen Victoria opened the Royal Border Bridge. Also known as the Berwick viaduct, it is one of the most stupendous structures on the ECML.

The 28-arch brick but stone-faced structure, designed by Robert Stephenson, crosses the Tweed, but not the border, which lies three miles to the north. It is 2162ft long and stands 124ft above the river. Grade I listed, it underwent significant repairs in the Nineties with the help of funding from English Heritage.

In 1847, the Newcastle & Berwick Railway merged with the York & Newcastle Railway to become the York, Newcastle and Berwick Railway.

The sole NER three-cylinder compound 4-4-0 No. 1619 working an Edinburgh-bound 'Scotch Express' past Benton Quarry in Newcastle. **TB PARLEY**

Inter-City High Speed Train No. 43113 forms the 1.35pm Edinburgh-Kings Cross service seen passing the Torness nuclear power station on September 9, 1987, before electrification masts were erected. **GAVIN MORRISON**

LNER A4 Pacific No. 60009 *Union of South Africa* heads the Railway Touring Company's 'Great Britain II' from Edinburgh to York on April 13, 2009. It is pictured here at Tweedmouth. **BRIAN SHARPE**

The western approach to Edinburgh Waverley station today. The Balmoral Hotel can be seen top left. **ROBIN JONES**

THE RISE OF
EDINBURGH WAVERLEY

In the steep narrow valley between Edinburgh's medieval Old Town and the 18th-century New Town lay a freshwater loch, the Nor Loch.

With the growth of the city, by the early 19th century it had become an open sewer, and was drained by 1820. When it was dry, much of the land was used to build the sprawling landscaped park named Princes Street Gardens.

Three stations appeared in the valley in the 1840s. The North British Railway opened North Bridge on June 22, 1846, followed by the Edinburgh & Glasgow's General station the following year. Also on May 17, 1847, the Edinburgh, Leith and Newhaven Railway opened its own station, Canal Street, also known as Edinburgh Princes Street.

All three stations came under the ownership of the North British in 1868. All of them were knocked down and the existing Edinburgh Waverley station was built in their place.

From the outset, it has been the most important station in the Scottish capital. In 1870, the Caledonian Railway opened another major station, also called Princes Street, but it never eclipsed Waverley, and closed in 1965.

In 1902, the North British built an imposing hotel next to Waverley to cater for travellers.

Sold by British Rail in 1983 to the Forte hotel group, it was upgraded and reopened in 1989 as the Balmoral Hotel, and today is one of the most luxurious in Britain. ∎

The main concourse at Edinburgh Waverley is very different to the facilities that were provided at the city's first railway station back in 1842. **ROBIN JONES**

CHAPTER THREE

Unique British Railways 8P Pacific No. 71000 *Duke of Gloucester* makes a storming departure from King's Cross on June 11, 2005, with the other forms of traction that use the station – diesel and electric – represented. **BRIAN SHARPE**

Next stop
Newcastle!

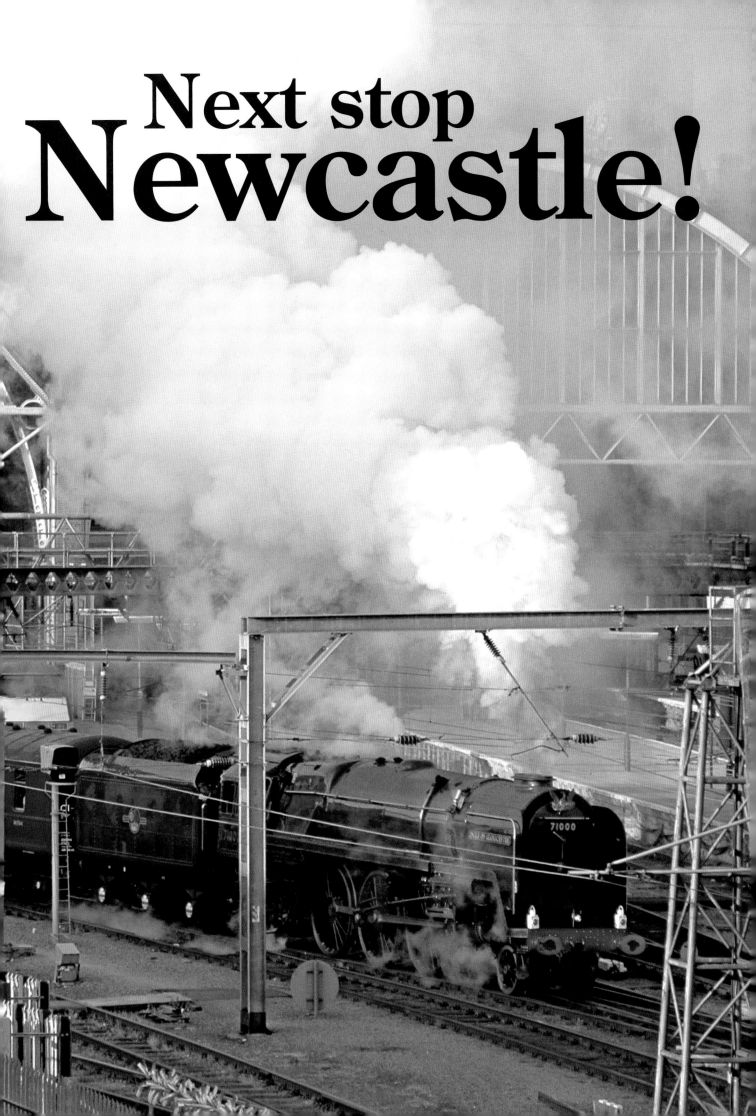

An immaculate A4 Pacific No 60028 *Walter K Whigham* stands at King's Cross on June 8, 1961, waiting to depart from beneath one of Lewis Cubbit's two great semi-circular roofs with the 10.15am Royal Train to York. **BRIAN MORRISON**

The gateway to the East Coast Main Line is London King's Cross, one of the most famous stations in the world, and justifiably so.

It is from here that examples of the world's fastest steam locomotives set out on their marathon journeys to the Scottish capital, reaching it in just over four hours, less than a tenth of the time it would have taken by stagecoach.

The first prospectus of the London & York Railway was issued on May 3, 1844, and plans were made for a main line from London to York, a loop line from Peterborough to Bawtry via Boston and Lincoln, and among other lines, a branch from Doncaster to Wakefield.

Despite fierce opposition from the London & Birmingham Railway and the Midland Railway, which had a monopoly of the existing traffic from London to Leeds and York, the London & York Bill finally received Royal Assent on June 26, 1846 as The Great Northern Railway Act 1846. The company took on the latter name, and had Leeds and York as its initial main targets.

Work began on building the Peterborough to Gainsborough section of the loop line first of all, because it was thought that as it crossed flat fenland it would be quicker and cheaper to build, and would start bringing in returns sooner. The GNR decided not to build the loop north of Gainsborough because it had been refused parliamentary powers for a branch from Bawtry to Sheffield, and instead

came to an arrangement with the Manchester Sheffield & Lincolnshire Railway to run over its line from Lincoln to GNR metals at Retford.

The first section of Great Northern Railway line was opened on March 1, 1848. It comprised the Grimsby to Louth section of the East Lincolnshire Railway, which the GNR leased from the outset.

The first section of track wholly owned by the GNR to be opened was the three-mile stretch from Doncaster to Askern Junction on October 1, 1848. At Askern Junction, the GNR line linked to the Lancashire & Yorkshire Railway route from Knottingley.

The East Lincolnshire line opened between Louth and Boston on October 1, 1848. Then 16 days later, the loop line between Werrington just north of Peterborough and Lincoln opened. Because the GNR main line had not yet been built, its trains used the Midland Railway's line to access Peterborough from Werrington Junction to Peterborough.

The GNR began running trains from Lincoln to Retford and on to Doncaster via the aforementioned Manchester Sheffield & Lincolnshire Railway (later Great Central) route on September 4, 1849.

Very quickly, the GNR gained its desired foothold in Leeds. On June 30, 1847, it agreed running rights over the Lancashire & Yorkshire from Askern Junction to Knottingley and on to Wakefield, and also from Knottingley to Methley on the Midland

Railway. From October 16 that year, the Midland permitted the GNR to run from Methley to Leeds.

Next stop would be York. The York & North Midland Railway agreed for the GNR to run trains over its line from Burton Salmon to York, and also over a new line from Knottingley to Burton Salmon, in return for the GNR promising not to build a line from Selby to York. The Knottingley to Burton Salmon route opened in June 1850.

THE LONDON GATEWAY

It was all going well in the East Midlands and south Yorkshire, but what about the most important part of the planned GNR trunk route, the section out of London?

William Cubitt was appointed as engineer-in-chief. A millwright, he had built up a reputation in civil engineering and had not only invented a new kind of windmill sail but the treadwheel that was notoriously used in Victorian prisons.

Before he came to London, he was chief engineer at the engineering firm of Ransomes in Ipswich, which later built steam-operated railway cranes.

He also worked on the South Eastern Railway, and in 1851, was the chief engineer of the Crystal Palace erected for the Great Exhibition.

William Cubitt's resident engineer for the GNR's London District was George Turnbull, who took command for the building of the first 20 miles of track out of the capital.

Turnbull, who was born near Perth, sailed from Dundee to London in 1828, a journey taking 41 hours by steam ship, to train under Thomas Telford while he was building St Katharine Docks in central London. In 1830 he was promoted to become Telford's draughtsman and clerk, and two years later surveyed new water supplies for London.

From 1840-42 Turnbull worked on building Middlesbrough Dock. It was later bought by the Stockton & Darlington Railway, the world's first public steam-operated line.

In 1843, he engineered the railway tunnel through Shakespeare Cliff between Dover and Folkestone, where he built a pier and landing stages.

Between 1846-49, he oversaw the building of the southernmost length of the GNR, including the Copenhagen, Tottenham, South Barnet, North Barnet and South Mimms tunnels and the many bridges en route.

At that stage, much of the line which is now in inner-city London ran through fields and open countryside.

At first, the line began from a temporary terminus at Maiden Lane north of the Regent's Canal, which opened on August 7, 1850 in time for the Great Exhibition. Officially named The London Temporary Passenger Station, it was surrounded by fields, brickworks and a fever hospital.

The station was a basic affair, comprising a trainshed made of cast and wrought iron, and which later saw used as a potato warehouse.

However, in 1848, Turnbull became involved with the planning of a terminus which would become an international byword for railway excellence – King's Cross.

Designed in detail by Lewis Cubitt, another member of the great family of civil engineers, this great 'cathedral of steam' was built during 1851–52 on the site of a former smallpox hospital.

It is easily the most imposing piece of GNR station architecture of all. That is remarkable especially in view of the fact that it had to be built quickly, as Maiden Lane was already showing signs of weakness.

Lewis Cubbit's design was based around a pair of 105ft glazed semi-circular roofs side by side, 800ft long and 72ft high. To speed up building work, the ribs were fabricated on site using laminated timber, but replaced in 1866 by more durable iron versions.

Between the roofs stood an Italianate clock turret, 120ft tall, from which three bells chimed until 1927.

Devoid of ornamentation, King's Cross was built for functionality, yet has an austere beauty of its own. When it was completed, its design was regarded as startling, yet it has certainly stood the test of time.

The station opened with just two platforms, against the east and west walls, and 14 tracks, most of which were used for storage only and could not be accessed from platforms. This original part includes today's platforms one to eight.

The station was one sided, with offices and passenger rooms situated on the west platform, which was used for departures. The east platform, which ran alongside York Way, handled arrivals only. There was no concourse, a much-later development.

Small turntables and capstans facilitated the movement of rolling stock without locomotive assistance.

To the north of the station, the railway passes beneath the canal, another feature for which Turnbull was responsible.

The original arrangement was outgrown within a few years, particularly after 1858 when the Midland Railway obtained permission to run services from Hitchin into King's Cross via the ECML on which GNR traffic levels continued to grow.

In the 1860s, tunnels were bored linking the GNR to the east-west Metropolitan Railway's Widened Lines. These included a platform on the Up curve under York Way and today carry the Thameslink services.

In 1875, a separate train shed was built with three suburban platforms, to accommodate the station's first commuter services, and this was extended in 1895. An island platform to the west was built in 1924.

Also in the 1870s, additional bores for the Gas Works and Copenhagen tunnels were dug. The tunnels immediately north the station have always been a bottleneck, limiting traffic movements between the stations, engine sheds, and freight yards.

While the new tunnels helped relieve congestion, in 1886 another double track bore was needed for Copenhagen Tunnel, and a third Gas Works Tunnel bore followed in 1892. That year, a second departure platform opened in the main station.

We think of King's Cross as a major passenger station, which today it exclusively is, but at the start it handled massive amounts of freight too. By the end of the 19th century it was handling a million tons of freight each year.

The GNR profited heavily from the capital's rapidly-growing needs for coal, vegetables, and meat, and vast amounts of sheep, pigs and cattle were shipped on a weekly basis, usually to the nearby Metropolitan Cattle Market.

Also, trainloads of coal were brought in from the Yorkshire-Nottinghamshire coalfield, and by late Victorian times, King's Cross boasted a sizeable coal depot.

In LNER days, pathing slow coal trains inbetween the fast expresses for which the ECML would become world famous presented a significant problem.

King's Cross (34A)-based A4 Pacific No. 60003 *Andrew K McCosh* blasts away from Copenhagen Tunnel on June 29, 1953 and starts the climb of Holloway Bank with 'The Norseman' express from King's Cross to Newcastle Tyne Commision Quay, carrying passengers for Norway. **BRIAN MORRISON**

The listed building near the site of the original King's Cross monument, with an ornamental lighthouse fixed on top.
ROBIN JONES

WHY 'KING'S CROSS'?

The name comes from a monument to King George IV that was built near the spot, at the junction of Gray's Inn Road, Pentonville Road and New Road (later Euston Road).

Standing 60ft tall with an 11ft statue of the monarch on top, it was completed in the mid-1830s.

The top floor was used as a camera obscura – offering sweeping views of the capital, while the bottom housed a police station and later a beer shop.

The monument attracted ridicule and was demolished in 1845, but the name that it had given to the locality stuck.

When the GNR built the grand terminus, some of its officials were aghast at the rundown nature of the locality in which it stood. The GNR's first goods manager, J Medcalf, described it as "a long battalion of rag sorters and cinder beaters".

The area had been settled by the Romans, and was later occupied by a village known as Battle Bridge. The focal point was Broad Ford Bridge, an ancient crossing of the River Fleet, which is now buried up to 40ft beneath London's streets and discharges its waters into the Thames below Blackfriars railway station.

It was long held that the name Battle Bridge derived from a major battle between the legions, who had a camp on this spot known as

The much-welcomed 1845 demolition of the King's Cross monument that gave the district its name. **ILLUSTRATED LONDON NEWS**

the Brill, and the Iceni tribe led by the warrior queen Boudica. An urban myth arose in the mid-20th century that Boudica is buried beneath platforms 9 or 10 at King's Cross.

Nearby is St Pancras Old Church, said to have been a site of Christian worship since AD314. It is dedicated to the Roman martyr St Pancras, beheaded at the age of 14 because he would not alter his beliefs. Largely rebuilt in Victorian times, it contains remnants of Norman features. It was superseded at the parish church by St Pancras New Church half a mile away in Euston Road, but remains as a green oasis sandwiched alongside two of Britain's busiest railway lines, those coming out of St Pancras International and King's Cross next door.

Around the 1870s, another landmark appeared near the site of the King's Cross. A lighthouse was erected on top of a building which today contains several boarded-up shops, sadly typical of the area around King's Cross in recent times, when it acquired notoriety for prostitution and drug abuse. Known locally as the Lighthouse Building, it is Grade II listed.

After his work on the GNR, in 1850 Turnbull was appointed chief engineer of the East Indian Railway and designed Calcutta's Howrah terminus and the 541-mile line to Benares on the road to Delhi.

The monument to Boudica on the Embankment at Westminster. Popular legend has it that she is buried under the platforms at King's Cross. **ROBIN JONES**

St Pancras Old Church, a green oasis just a stone's throw from King's Cross. **ROBIN JONES**

King's Cross was originally a bridging point on the River Fleet. **ROBIN JONES**

Gasworks Tunnel is the first tunnel on the ECML leading directly out of the station throat of King's Cross. **ROBIN JONES**

The front of King's Cross station as seen in the 1920s. An assortment of huts can be seen in the station forecourt, together with a stairwell entrance to King's Cross St Pancras Underground station, Northern and Piccadilly lines. **LONDON TRANSPORT MUSEUM**

The exterior of King's Cross station as built, showing Lewis Cubitt's great façade. **ILLUSTRATED LONDON NEWS**

TOO HIGH FOR A QUEEN

One of William Cubitt's greatest legacies on the ECML is the great Welwyn or Digswell viaduct, which carries the GNR route over the River Mimram, just to the south of Welwyn North station.

The 40-arch viaduct spans around 1560ft and towers 100ft above the ground. Built from bricks made from clay quarried on the site itself, it took two years to build. Cubitt designed it in the style of a Roman aqueduct.

It was opened by Queen Victoria on August 6, 1850, but she was scared of its height and refused to travel across it. Her train had to stop so she could disembark and travel the length of the viaduct by a horse-drawn carriage, rejoining the train at the other end.

It is a truly magnificent structure, but a severely-limited one too. It carries just two tracks, so the four-line ECML has to narrow down at this point. The bottleneck is further exacerbated by the position of Welwyn north station at its northern end.

With today's increasing demand for space on the ECML, the problem of the viaduct is regularly discussed, but the money to build a second alongside has yet to be forthcoming.

The great Welwyn Viaduct is in itself a magnificent engineering structure, but presents major problems as a bottleneck. **JASON ROGERS/CREATIVE COMMONS**

THE LONDON TERMINUS OPENS

The GNR main line from Maiden Lane to Peterborough via Biggleswade and Huntingdon opened on August 7, 1850. In Newcastle Central station, a great banquet was held to mark the occasion, for it meant that a new fast through route from London to Edinburgh was completed.

There were eight trains leaving London to the north, via Peterborough and the Lincolnship loop. First of all, a 6am service ran all stations to Knottingly, and then express to York: it was the only one that carried third class passengers, and took 11 hours and four minutes to reach Doncaster.

At 7.40am, there was the 'Scotch Express' which ran to York, where connections would be made for trains to Edinburgh. It took seven hours and 10 minutes.

At 10.30am, there was an express to Leeds and York.

The noon train ran all stations to Hitchin, the 2pm service all stations to Doncaster (which took eight hours 10 minutes) and the 5pm all stations to Peterborough. There was a 6pm express to Leeds and York and an 8pm train running all stations to Hitchin.

Between London and Peterborough, there were stations at Hornsey, Colney Hatch & Southgate, Barnet, Potters Bar, Hatfield, Welwyn, Stevenage, Hitchin, Arlseley & Shefford Road, Biggleswade, Sandy, St Neots, Huntingdon and Holme.

From Peterborough, the line followed the already-built GNR route to Spalding, Boston and Lincoln to Retford.

In August 1851, Victoria and her consort Prince Albert travelled from Maiden Lane to Scotland via the GNR, boosting its soaring popularity.

However, it was clear from the outset that it was a long-winded way of reaching York, greater than that of the rival Midland Railway's route from London to York. The missing link between Peterborough and Retford had to be completed and fast. The latter word would within a century add more than a touch of irony.

Sandy station lies 44 miles north of King's Cross and was built for the GNER in 1850, opening with the rest of the line on August 7 that year. The LNWR opened an adjacent station in 1862, but the pair were later merged into one, sharing the island platform. The station is now served by a half-hourly service southbound to King's Cross and northbound to Peterborough, with an hourly service each way on Sundays. **ROBIN JONES**

The Great Northern Hotel opposite the entrance to Peterborough station. **ROBIN JONES**

The girder bridge over the River Nene at Peterborough was designed by Lewis Cubitt, the architect for King's Cross station. LMS Princess Coronation Pacific No. 6233 *Duchess of Sutherland* is seen heading a southbound railtour. **BRIAN SHARPE**

Complete with 'Scarborough Flyer' headboard, the Up express is shown passing under the old Great North Road as it heads out of Grantham and climbs towards Stoke Summit with King's Cross-based Gresley V2 No. 60862 on September 5, 1959. **GAVIN MORRISON**

THE CONQUEST OF STOKE BANK

William Cubitt's son Joseph was appointed engineer-in-chief for the Peterborough to Retford line.

The first 5½ miles saw it follow the Midland Railway's line from Leicester as far as Helpston, from where it had to tackle the great limestone ridge that extends in a line across England from the Cotswolds to the Lincolnshire Wolds.

However, unlike the Midland line, the GNR route to the north bypassed Stamford, the one-time great coaching town.

In 1847, the parliamentary election in Stamford was fought over the GNR route. Several requests had been made to build the line through Stamford, giving it a new direct connection to London superseding the Great North Road.

However, there were three petitions against such a deviation, one the Midland Railway and two from landowners the Earl of Lindsay and the Marquess of Exeter on the grounds of residential injury.

On November 1, 1856, a four-mile long line, the Stamford & Essendine Railway, built with the support of the second Marquis of Exeter, finally linked the town to the GNR, but only as a branch.

From Tallington, on the edge of the flat Cambridgeshire fens, the line rose slowly up the ridge, at the start of what has become known as Stoke Bank, and is legendary with

great reason in railway circles.

Bypassing the village of Greatford, there was the aforementioned station at Essendine, which also became junction for a line serving the market town of Bourne, Little Bytham, where the Midland & Great Northern Junction Railway crossed at right angles on the level above, and to Stoke Summit, at 380ft the highest point on the ECML, and roughly 100 miles from King's Cross. The 1-in-178 climb from Corby Glen for the three miles to the summit is the steepest on any part of the route north of Holloway.

Beyond Stoke Tunnel, which takes the line through part of the ridge while beginning the descent from the summit, the gradient is 1-in-200 as the route descends into the Trent valley.

Indeed, Stoke Bank is the only major gradient on the GNR line, which followed a fairly straight course from London to the point, paving the way for speeds to be increase as locomotive technology developed.

Next stop is Grantham, which became important as a halfway point between London and York, and the junction for the GNR branch to Nottingham.

Beyond Grantham is Peascliffe Tunnel and Barkston, from where in 1867 a branch to Lincoln was opened.

At Newark-on-Trent, the GNR crossed its rival the Midland on the level. Today, the flat crossing is one of only two on the national

network, the other being the point on the Cambrian coast line at Porthmadog where the reinstated 2ft gauge Welsh Highland Railway crosses the Network Rail line. Such flat crossings were not rare in the steam age in UK, and many can be seen on the continent, but in terms of standard gauge, this one is unique.

The GNR opted for the flat crossing rather than a bridge not only to save money but because the River Trent had also to be crossed a short distance beyond. The crossing was controlled by a signalbox on the Midland line from the outset until 1948.

Beyond there the line briefly parallels the Great North Road, and then comes Dukeries Junction where the GNR bisected the Manchester, Sheffield & Lincolnshire Railway.

Just before Retford, there was, until 1965, a second flat crossing, where the GNR crossed the Sheffield & Lincolnshire Junction Railway, later Manchester, Sheffield & Lincolnshire Railway, which had taken the first GNR from the Lincolnshire loop line from Peterborough via Boston and Lincoln.

Today Retford has high level platforms serving the ECML and low level ones for the Sheffield to Lincoln line, which was lowered in 1965 to pass beneath the ECML.

The missing link between Peterborough and Retford was completed in 1852 and King's Cross opened on October 14 that year.

ONWARDS TO LEEDS

The Leeds, Bradford & Halifax Junction Railway opened between Leeds and Bowling Junction near Bradford on August 1, 1854. By exercising its running powers both over this line and a section of the Lancashire & Yorkshire Railway, the GNR obtained access to Bradford and Halifax.

The West Yorkshire Railway opened its direct line from Wakefield to Leeds via Ardsley in 1857. As the GNR already had running powers over this line, it began using it and ditched the Midland route via Methley.

The Manchester, Sheffield & Lincolnshire Railway allowed the GNR to run a London to Manchester via Retford service over its metals, and GNR trans also ran to Huddersfield via Penistone from 1859.

In 1867, the final piece of the Lincolnshire loop line was built by the GNR, and created a junction with the new main line at Black Carr, eliminating the need for GNR trains to run over the Manchester, Sheffield & Lincolnshire to Retford.

The GNR main line ended at Shaftholme, a small hamlet two north of Doncaster, described as in "a ploughed field".

However, it was there that it had an end-on junction with the North Eastern Railway, which had come into existence in 1854 through the amalgamation of four companies in the York Newcastle & Berwick, the York & North Midland, the Leeds Northern and the Malton & Driffield Junction railways.

It was the NER that comprised the middle section of the jigsaw in the great rail route from London to Edinburgh.

The opening of a direct line from Shaftholme Junction to York via Selby in January 1871 saw the end of regular express trains using the Askern route from Shaftholme to Knottingly, the branch to Burton Salmon and the York & North Midland Railway's line from Normanton to York. It was also one of a series of periodic shortenings of the ECML's middle section which has persisted up to recent times.

YORK TO DARLINGTON AND NEWCASTLE

The idea of building a York to Newcastle railway dated back to 1835. George Stephenson surveyed the route and the scheme was backed by Edward Pease of the Stockton & Darlington Railway. The Newcastle-Darlington section received Royal Assent in 1836 and the York-Darlington section a year later.

It had been planned to build the Newcastle-Darlington section first, but work began on the southern part of the line at Croft and the York to Darlington section opened on March 30, 1841.

The line incorporated a mineral branch of the Stockton & Darlington from Albert Hill Junction, which passed through the area now occupied by Darlington station.

The company had exhausted all its funds, and so another was formed to build the Newcastle to Darlington section. The Newcastle & Darlington Junction Railway continued the new main line northwards towards Ferryhill and Newcastle, opening it on June 19, 1844.

Railway magnate George Hudson angered the Stockton & Darlington by refusing to include part of it into the new route, and eventually got his way. Hudson was also involved in the Newcastle-Berwick-Edinburgh line, having had his York & North Midland Railway invest £50,000 in the North British Railway. Hudson is said to have used unscrupulous methods to add the Great North of England Railway to his vast portfolio of lines.

However, Hudson became embroiled in scandal and was ruined by the disclosure of fraud in the Eastern Railway, along with the discovery of his bribery of MPs. By 1850, his influence on the railway sector had vanished.

As it was, the York to Newcastle railway crossed the Stockton & Darlington via a flat crossing at Parkgate Junction which would over ensuing decades become a nightmare for both the North Eastern railway and its successors.

Darlington station, also known as Darlington Bank Top, was originally a basic affair which was rebuilt in 1860 to cope with the increase in traffic.

It too was superseded within 20 years when the NER constructed a stylish new station with an three-span trainshed roof. The improvements also included a new connecting line from the south end of the station to meet the original Stockton & Darlington route towards Middlesbrough at Oak Tree Junction.

It is understood that Queen Victoria expressed the view that Darlington deserved a better station. The scheme was completed on July 1, 1887, after which Darlington became a busy ECML junction with routes to Bishop Auckland, Richmond, Barnard Castle and Penrith via Stainmore Summit and Saltburn diverging.

The centre of York station was the Zero Point for the measurement of 10 of the North Eastern Railway's lines, including those to Newcastle, Beverley, Harrogate, Scarborough and Normanton. This replica at the station was erected by the North Eastern Railway Trust with help from the Railway Heritage Trust and the Ken Hoole Trust, and unveiled by multi-millionaire enthusiast and former *Flying Scotsman* owner Sir William McAlpine, chairman of the NERT, to mark the 150th anniversary to the date of the formation of the NER on July 31, 1854. **ROBIN JONES**

York station as depicted in 1877.

YORK BECOMES A THROUGH STATION

York was the initiation destination for GNR trains from London when the line opened in 1850. It was there that passengers could change for Scotland.

The first railway station at York was opened in 1839 by the York & North Midland Railway in a temporary wooden building in Queen Street, outside the city walls.

It was replaced from January 4, 1841, inside the walls by an Italianate-style terminus built at the junction of Toft Green, Tanner Row and Station Rise and designed by the company's architect George Townsend Andrews. He also designed the neo-Tudor arch where the city walls were breached to allow the railway in.

Andrews also designed the Royal Station Hotel, completed in 1853 and named as such following a visit by Victoria.

It was the first hotel in the world to be incorporated into a railway station.

With the arrival of other lines, York became a primary point on the ECML. However, through trains were forced to reverse out of the station to continue their journeys, and so a new station was built and opened in 1877, this time outside the city walls again. Designed by NER architects Thomas Prosser and William Peachey with its magnificent trainshed roof, it was at the time the biggest station in the world, having 13 platforms.

The following year, the Royal Station Hotel, also designed by Peachey, was opened.

The redundant old station and hotel were converted into offices, while tracks remained in use as carriage sidings.

In February 2010, the City of York Council announced that it intended to convert the station into its new 150,000 sq ft headquarters.

Freight traffic was far more important at King's Cross in the steam era than today. Restarting from a signal check at Darlington, the regular heavy train of fish vans from Aberdeen to King's Cross is hauled by Class A2/3 Pacific No 60512 *Steady Aim* on May 20, 1959. **BRIAN MORRISON**

The huge curving junction on which York station rests. The station can be seen in the bottom right of the picture, with the National Railway Museum, marked by the now-dismantled York Eye viewing wheel, to its upper left. The ECML from Doncaster enters the picture bottom left, and curves away to the top right, while the Scarborough branch leaves York on the right. **NETWORK RAIL**

Flying Scotsman leaves York with its magnificent trainshed roof in 2004, following its purchase by the National Railway Museum, en route to Scarborough. **BRIAN SHARPE**

NEWCASTLE CENTRAL

Another crucial link in the connection of the English and Scottish railway systems was the building of the High Level bridge over the River Tyne at Newcastle.

Designed by Robert Stephenson, it was built for the York, Newcastle & Berwick Railway between 1847-49 and is the first major example of a wrought iron tied arch or bowstring girder bridge.

Spanning 1337ft, its has stands up to 131ft above the river. There are six spans over the river and four on land.

Single carriageway road and pedestrian walkways occupy the lower deck of the spans, and the railway the upper deck.

Its completion enabled trains to run from London to Edinburgh for the first time. Rail traffic began using it on August 15, 1849, but it was officially opened on September 27 that year by Queen Victoria.

In many respects it is an improved version of Stephenson's Britannia Bridge over the Menai Strait.

In 1906, the King Edward VII Bridge 500 yards upstream was completed. This solved the main problem of the High Level Bridge in that trains entering Newcastle Centre station from the south had to be reversed back across the bridge when returning in that direction. Also, engines had to switch ends before a train

could head north towards Edinburgh.

The opening of the new bridge led to it becoming part of the ECML, with the High Level Bridge downgraded to handling local services to Sunderland, Middlesbrough and the Leamside Line.

Many regard the vast curving Newcastle Central as the finest station in England. It was designed by John Dobson, in his day the most famous architect in the north.

He exhibited his original plans for the station at the Paris Exhibition of 1858, where they won an award, but he was asked to scale down the grandiose design to cut costs.

Although the station was completed in 1850, with a neoclassical-styled frontage, the

façade portico, subsequently designed by Thomas Prosser, was not added for another 13 years.

Plans for an Italianate tower were also dropped. However, the station was widely acclaimed for its three great arched roofs built in a curve on an 800ft radius to form a trainshed. It was described as the first large glass and iron vault in England.

The station was built in collaboration with Stephenson, Queen Victoria officially opened it on August 29, 1850.

The train shed was extended southwards in the 1890s with a new span designed by William Bell.

Robert Stephenson's High Level Bridge across the Tyne, with the road swing bridge in the foreground. **TAGISHSIMON/CREATIVE COMMONS**

Gresley A3 No. 4472 *Flying Scotsman* heads a special from Newcastle across Plawsworth Viaduct near Chester-le-Street in County Durham on September 14, 1975. Subsequent growth of vegetation makes this view difficult to photograph nowadays. **GAVIN MORRISON**

A Class 47 heads a service to Edinburgh out of Newcastle Central over the diamond crossing in British Rail days. The tracks to the left run to Sunderland while to the right, the ECML continues to Berwick. **GAVIN MORRISON**

LEAMSIDE:
THE FORGOTTEN MAIN LINE

When it was completed in 1850, parts of the ECML followed a very different route to that which we know today.

One such section is the Leamside line in County Durham, running from Ferryhill in the south to Pelaw in the north.

The Leamside line came into existence in piecemeal fashion when several shorter routes were joined up to form a main line.

The first section used by passenger trains was that from Washington to Rainton Meadows south of Fencehouses in March 1840, having opened to freight in August 1838.

This line was operated by the Durham Junction Railway, with expectations of a link to the Hartlepool Dock & Railway Company, but this failed to happen, and it left Rainham Meadows as the southern terminus of the route from Tyneside.

In 1844, the Durham Junction Railway became part of the Newcastle & Darlington Junction Railway, which aimed to connect both towns in its title.

The northern section from Washington to Pelaw, incorporating part of the Stanhope & Tyne Railway, was joined with the southern sections to the south, from Rainton Crossing to Shincliffe and to Ferryhill. At Pelaw Junction, the line joined the Newcastle to Sunderland route.

The biggest engineering structure on the line is the stupendous 10-arch Victoria Viaduct, which spans the River Wear and was so named because the last stone was laid on June 28, 1838, Queen Victoria's Coronation Day.

The completed route was opened to passenger traffic in June 1844, but as with many railways in Durham, mineral traffic was the main source of revenue, mainly in the form of local coal.

The route was streamlined in 1849 when a more direct line between Washington and Pelaw via Usworth opened to freight, and was used by passenger trains from October 1850, doubling up as the ECML between Newcastle and Darlington, joining today's route south towards York at Tursdale Junction.

A new route from Durham to Newcastle was opened by the North Eastern Railway in 1872, and it is this section, not the Leamside line, which forms part of the ECML today.

The Leamside line remained as an alternative route and for local stopping trains at the intermediate stations of Usworth, Washington, Penshaw, Fence Houses, Leamside, Sherburn colliery, Shincliffe and Ferryhill. Freight remained of paramount importance; at Washington, iron ore trains would be marshalled for the long haul up to Consett steelworks.

The first passenger closure came in July 1941 with the Leamside-Ferryhill service, while once-busy Leamside station was shut in October 1953 and demolished.

The Beeching Report of 1963 identified the Leamside line for withdrawal of passenger trains, but conceded it had a future for freight. All regular services between Pelaw and Fencehouses, along with the short western link to Durham and Penshaw-

Parts of the original ECML such as the Leamside section were bypassed as early as Victorian times. Just a year before it was closed in October 1953, racing pigeon owners prepare to load their birds on to a pigeon van at Leamside station for conveyance to London.
BEAMISH MUSEUM

Commissioned by the Durham Junction Railway, the Victoria Viaduct which carried the Leamside line over the River Wear was built between 1836 and 1838 to a Thomas Elliot Harrison design based on the Roman bridge at Alcántara in Spain. **PETER HUGHES/CREATIVE COMMONS**

Sunderland section, ended in May 1964. It remained in use for freight and also as a diversionary route, last being used as such during the electrification of the ECML.

The gradual demise of the Durham coalfield in the Seventies and Eighties led to a sharp fall in freight traffic, and the Leamside closed to all through traffic in 1991, following the closure of the Freightliner terminal at Follingsby near Washington,

The line was not ripped up, as was the usual practice under British Railways in the Sixties and Seventies, but mothballed, because of its potential to serve new opencast workings.

A report commissioned by the Tyne and Wear Passenger Transport Authority suggested in 2008 that the Leamside line could be reborn to provide a regional service linking the Tees Valley and Tyne and Wear regions, running from Newcastle Central. However, parts of the line have since been lifted while others are buried by vegetation. ■

Thomas Bouch's ill-fated
original Tay Bridge.

The Forth Bridge has stood the test of time for
more than 120 years, and Network Rail believes
that it will be good for at least another century.
A railtour hauled by LNER K4 2-6-0 No. 61994
The Great Marquess is pictured having just
crossed it. **BRIAN SHARPE.**

Two bridges to Aberdeen

T he East Coast Main Line proper is officially the route from King's Cross to Edinburgh Waverley and from Doncaster to Leeds.

However, the Edinburgh to Aberdeen route is often grouped together with the ECML, if only in referring to through services from London.

The route to Aberdeen did play a significant part in the ECML becoming the world's fastest steam line, and so a digression to the Granite City comes within the scope of this book. By the mid-1860s, the North British Railway was running main line trains to Berwick, Carlisle, Glasgow and Aberdeen.

The latter was achieved via the Edinburgh & Northern Railway, later the Edinburgh, Perth & Dundee Railway, which ran from Burntisland on the northern shore of the Firth of Forth. It operated services between Burntisland, on the northern and Tayport, from where a boat took passengers to Broughty Ferry for onwards travel to Dundee and Aberdeen.

When it began operating on February 3, 1850, the ferry from Burntisland to Granton was the world's first railway ferry.

The railway became part of the North British on July 29, 1862.

Needless to say, the Aberdeen route was an awkward and finicky affair, and it involved two crossings of major river estuaries, those of the Forth and the Tay.

Passengers were taken across both by ferries, and the final 28 miles into Aberdeen were achieved only by way of running rights over the Caledonian Railway's line from Kinnaber Junction.

The North British route was the shorter, but far less convenient than the Caledonian counterpart from Edinburgh to Aberdeen, which went around the heads of both estuaries.

There was only one solution: bridge the Tay and the Forth.

THE LONGEST RAILWAY BRIDGE IN THE WORLD

Thomas Bouch was appointed designer and overseer for the Tay crossing project.

Bouch had already built up an outstanding reputation. He helped develop the caisson, a watertight structure for use in bridge pier building and ship repairs, and also the roll-on roll-off train ferry. For the North British, he designed parts of Edinburgh Waverley station, and also built bridges on the long-closed Stainmore route across the Pennines.

He first approached the Edinburgh & Northern Railway in 1854 about bridging the Tay, but the capital was not forthcoming. A decade later he was working on plans to cross both the Tay and the Forth.

In 1869, the Tay Bridge scheme was revived as a separate undertaking. The North British invested heavily in it, despite public fears that a two-mile crossing of the sea could not be built and if it was, it would not last. The company's shareholders, however, backed it fully.

The foundation stone was laid on July 22, 1871 and the bridge was built to a design using a lattice grid that combined wrought and cast iron. Building work progressed slowly; on January 19, 1877, two spans were blown down in a gale.

The first train ran over the single-track bridge on September 26, 1877, carrying local VIPs and senior railway officials. It was inspected by the Board of Trade in late February 1878 and passed, and carried its first fare-paying passengers on June 1, 1878. At one mile and 1705 yards, the 88ft tall structure was the longest railway bridge in the world.

Efforts to find victims of the Tay Bridge disaster were in vain.

It was an enormous boost for the North British Railway, which afterwards attracted 84% of the Edinburgh to Dundee traffic, and the bridge attracted rich and famous visitors from far and wide. Queen Victoria crossed it in 1879 – no fears this time as had been the case with the Welwyn Viaduct, and knighted Bouch – who around the same time began building a second bridge, that crossing the Forth at Queensferry.

However, one of the worst disasters in British railway history occurred on December 28, 1879, when a Beaufort force 10/11 gale beset the east coast of Scotland.

The Tay Bridge took the full force of strong side winds and the central section, known as the 'High Girders', collapsed, taking a train of six coaches with it.

All 75 passengers on board, some of them having travelled from King's Cross, died. Only 46 of the bodies were ever found, while some were never identified. The actual number of victims was established by painstaking examination of ticket sales.

The disaster sent shock waves both through the country and the Victorian civil engineering sector.

The rebuilt Tay Bridge today. **NETWORK RAIL**

A Court of Inquiry was set up in a bid to establish the reason for the collapse. It found that "the fall of the bridge was occasioned by the insufficiency of the cross bracing and its fastenings to sustain the force of the gale." The court said that if the piers, and in particular the wind bracing, had been properly constructed and maintained, the bridge could have withstood the storm that night, albeit with reduced safety levels.

Bouch's choice of cast iron as a building material was seriously questioned.

The inquiry concluded that the bridge was "badly designed, badly built and badly maintained."

Bouch's reputation was in shreds. He was mainly blamed for the collapse in not making sufficient allowance for wind loading. There was also evidence that the central structure had been deteriorating for several months before the disaster, with indications that joints had loosened.

As a direct result, the design of the Forth railway bridge was quickly transferred to Sir Benjamin Baker and Sir John Fowler.

Bouch's hopes of being allowed to rebuild the bridge were understandably dashed.

The new steel bridge was built under the direction of William Henry Barlow, who had engineered the Midland Railway's London extension and designed its London terminus at St Pancras. He also helped completed Isambard Kingdom Brunel's Clifton Suspension Bridge four years after the Great Western Railway engineer died.

He sat on the commission which investigated the causes of the Tay Bridge disaster and designed the replacement, with his son Crawford Barlow as engineer. The new design used large monocoque piers to support a double track railway. The brick and masonry piers from the first bridge were kept as breakwaters for the new piers upstream.

Building started in 1882 and the new stronger bridge was opened on July 13, 1887.

Thomas Bouch died a few months after the public inquiry into the disaster ended, his health having severely deteriorated.

The locomotive, North British Railway 4-4-0 No. 224 which had been built at Cowlairs in 1871, was eventually recovered from the estuary, rebuilt and returned to service. It remained in service until 1919, and was nicknamed 'The Diver'. However, several superstitious drivers refused to take it over the replacement bridge.

A MARVEL OF CIVILISATION

The North British had seen only too well the immense value of bridging the 'unbridgeable' and was determined to add a second bridge to its empire, across the Forth.

Bouch had proposed a suspension bridge and the scheme reached the point where the foundation stone was laid. However, the inquiry's findings that his Tay Bridge had been under strength stopped the project.

Instead, Fowler and Baker came up with a cantilever design, the first bridge in Britain to be made entirely from steel.

It was built by the Glasgow firm of Sir William Arrol & Company between 1883-90.

However, during its construction, more than 450 of the estimated 4600 workers were injured and 98 lost their lives, a death toll which exceeded that of the Tay bridge disaster.

Nonetheless, the Forth railway bridge was, and still is, regarded as one of the greatest engineering achievements in the history of civilisation.

Stretching 1.6 miles from North to South Queensferry, main crossing comprises tubular struts and lattice girder ties in double cantilevers each connected by 345ft 'suspended' girder spans resting on the cantilever ends. It has two 1710ft main spans of 521.3 metres, two side spans of 680ft and 15 approach spans each 168ft long. Standing 151ft above high tide and weighing 50,513 tons, it used nearly 65,000 tons of steel,

18,122 cu. metres of granite and 6.5 million rivets. Where possible, natural features were incorporated into the design for added stability, such as the island of Inchgarvie, and the headlands and high banks on either side.

The double track bridge was officially completed on March 4, 1890 when the Prince of Wales, the future Edward VII, tapped an inscribed golden rivet into position.

The bridge cost a total of £3,200,000, nearer to £235 million by today's standards.

Bettering the routes to Aberdeen offered by the Caledonian, it provided a huge boost to the fortunes of the North British, but it was not owned outright by that company. A conference at York in 1881 had set up the Forth Bridge Railway Committee, to which the North British agreed to meet 35% of the cost. The Midland Railway agreed to contribute 30%, while the rest came equally from North Eastern Railway and the Great Northern Railway. As with the East Coast Joint Stock, it was yet another example of the very close co-operation that led to the eventual unification of services on the ECML.

On October 16, 1939, the first Luftwaffe attack on Britain during the Second World War took place over the bridge, when Nazi bombers attacked the Royal Navy base at Rosyth. The incident also saw the first German planes to be shot down over Britain during the conflict, thanks to the RAF 603 City of Edinburgh Spitfire squadron. ∎

LNER A4 Pacific No. 4488 *Union of South Africa* crossing the Forth Bridge with an Aberdeen-Edinburgh express in 1940. **THE RAILWAY MAGAZINE**

An aerial view of a National Express High Speed Train crossing the first section of the Forth Bridge in 2007. **EAST COAST**

The Forth Bridge, one of the greatest engineering marvels of the Victorian age, illuminated at night. **NETWORK RAIL**

CHAPTER FIVE

Sturrock:
starting the quest for speed

A panoramic view of 'The Plant' at Doncaster, which originated in Sturrock's day, and the north end of the station, with Deltic No. 55008 *The Green Howards* leaving on the 8am King's Cross-Edinburgh service on July 7, 1977. **GAVIN MORRISON**

T he GNR appointed engineer Benjamin Cubitt as its first locomotive superintendent, but his only contribution was to order 40 2-2-2s from Sharp Brothers, but died before he saw any train run.

He was replaced by Edward Bury, already a seasoned and respected locomotive engineer. He also had other interests, especially in Bury, Curtis & Kennedy locomotive builders. However, the GNR was not satisfied that his locomotives were suitable for its operation and removed him.

The next superintendent, Archibald Sturrock, was a 34-year-old Scot recruited from the Great Western Railway, where he had briefly been works manager at Swindon under Daniel Gooch in broad gauge days, and came with a letter of recommendation from Isambard Kingdom Brunel.

At the time, locomotive boilers were usually pressed to no more than 100lb/sq in, but Sturrock thought differently. He was not content to continue the GNR policy of buying engines from outside contractors, but wanted to design and build his own. His first engine and others that followed had a working pressure of 150lb/sq in. He was a great believer in large fireboxes and grate areas to produce easy-to-fire free-steaming boilers. Ahead of his time in many ways, Sturrock was very much influenced by the Swindon designs of the day, even though he would have to adapt them from 7ft ¼in to 4ft 8½in gauge.

Sturrock was told by the GNR board to produce locomotives that could fill one primary objective. Speed. His achievement was not only the opening of the GNR main line but its reputation for a reliable and quality service from King's Cross north.

Sturrock and most of the board wanted to build his locomotive workshops at Peterborough. The GNR's first locomotive and carriage repair shops were built in 1848 at Boston in Lincolnshire, but it became clear that the premises would be quickly outgrown as traffic increased.

However, chairman Edmund Denison championed Doncaster as the home of any new workshops, and in 1851 won the day. The works was established on July 24, 1852, and 700 staff were transferred from Boston. By December, it had 949 men working there.

When Sturrock came to the GNR, it had 150 locomotives. By 1866, 282 had been built to his designs – but it was not until the following year that Doncaster turned out its first locomotive.

He also produced some outstanding coaches which were all but exclusively used on Anglo-Scottish expresses, and even produced a 4-2-2, No. 215, which he hoped in vain could run from King's Cross to Edinburgh in eight hours, claiming it could reach 75mph.

Because of the flimsy rails of the GNR, Sturrock experimented with steam tenders. One of his 0-6-0 types had a tender which was powered by two 12in by17in cylinders, in addition to two 16in by 24in locomotive cylinders. It was a means of producing a more powerful engine but not a heavier one.

The type proved unreliable, and unpopular with firemen, and the concept ended up being a cul-de-sac in locomotive design as it was eventually discontinued. Some believe that it may have contributed to Sturrock parting company with the GNR in 1866, when he supposedly retired after marrying into wealth.

While the GNR did not build any of Sturrock's engines itself, and hired contractors to do the job, during his retirement in Doncaster, Sturrock helped found locomotive builder the Yorkshire Engine Company and became its chairman for several years. He died in London in 1909.

The GNR engine repair shops at 'The Plant'.

One of three Sturrock 264 class 2-40s, No. 266 is seen at the John Fowler & Co works in Leeds when completed in 1866. Three further examples were built by the Yorkshire Engine Company, of which Sturrock became chairman after leaving the GNR.

THE TWO GREAT WORKS

Two locomotive building workshops will forever by synonymous with the East Coast Main Line: Doncaster and Darlington.

Doncaster Works has always been known as 'The Plant'. Until 1867 it undertook only repairs and maintenance before building its first locomotive.

In the mid-Eighties, under Sturrock's successor Patrick Stirling, it began building new coaches, and the first sleeping cars were outshopped there in 1873.

Doncaster built Britain's first dining cars in 1879, and the first corridor coaches followed three years later.

This volume is devoted to the story of how the ECML became a byword for speed, and to cut a long story short, most of the groundbreaking locomotives classes that ran over it and wowed the world were built at Doncaster. They included, as we will see in the chapters that follow, the Stirling Singles, the Ivatt Atlantics and the Gresley Pacifics, including No. 4472 *Flying Scotsman* and the streamlined A4s.

During the Second World War, Doncaster turned out Horsa gliders for the D-Day airborne assault. In British Railways days, it produced the new BR standard all-steel Mk1 carriages.

Steam building ended in 1957, followed by carriage building in 1962. However, the works were yanked into the modern age with the building of a diesel repair shop.

Under British Rail Engineering Limited, new diesels and electric locomotives have been built. Celebrations were held in July 2003 to mark its 150th birthday.

Sadly, in 2008 the main locomotive repair shop was demolished to make way for housing.

The Stockton & Darlington Railway opened Darlington Works in 1863.

The first new locomotive was built there in 1864, to a S&D design. It was not for another four years that North Eastern Railway designs were turned out.

At the works, known locally as North Road Shops, 120 of Sir Vincent Raven's Q6 0-8-0s had been built by 1921, followed by 15 examples of the more powerful Q7 0-8-0s. After the Grouping, it built Gresley's K3 2-6-0s, V2 2-6-2s, K4 2-6-0s and A1 Pacifics.

Steam building continued until after nationalisation, with BR Standard Class 2 tanks being turned out. Despite being enlarged in 1954, rationalisation of the BR Workshops Division in 1962 saw the works run down and closed four years later. The site is now occupied by a Morrisons supermarket… but as we shall see, express passenger steam locomotive building for the ECML in Darlington did not die forever. ∎

An exhibition of steam locomotives was held in the bay platforms at the north end of Darlington station during the Stockton & Darlington Railway 150 year celebrations, with A4 No. 4498 *Sir Nigel Gresley* and LNER K1 2-6-0 No. 2005 pictured on August 21, 1975. A Peak class diesel is seen leaving with a train for Newcastle. **GAVIN MORRISON**

The original GNR workshops at Boston are now a health and fitness club. **BRIAN SHARPE**

CHAPTER SIX

Single-minded Stirling

When Patrick Stirling was appointed to the Great Northern Railway as locomotive superintendent in 1866, he had speed as his aim. He wanted new standard engines which combined speed with power in order to tackle the continuous gradients on the King's Cross to York line.

The most famous of his locomotives were the Stirling Singles, 4-2-2s with distinctive 8ft 1in driving wheels and domeless boilers, nicknamed 'eight footers', and they became distinctive images of Victorian railway technology at its finest… and fastest.

Stirling, who was born in Kilmarnock in 1820, came from a family that had already made its mark in steam engineering. His father, the Reverend Robert Stirling, had four years earlier invented the first practical example of a closed cycle air engine in 1816, and they later came to be known as Stirling engines. His brother James Stirling was also a locomotive engineer, while Patrick's son Matthew became chief mechanical engineer of the Hull & Barnsley Railway.

Patrick Stirling was taken on as an apprentice at Urquhart Lindsay & Company's Dundee Foundry and subsequently became foreman at Neilson's Locomotive Works in Glasgow.

In 1851, he became superintendent of a short line between Bowling and Balloch which was later taken over the North British Railway. Two years later, he was made locomotive superintendent of the Glasgow & South Western Railway where he stayed for 13 years.

His finest hour, however, came at the GNR, where he stayed in charge until his death in 1895.

He disliked the concept of compound engines, and preferred traditional types with outside cylinders and domeless boilers.

One of his first moves at the GNR was to borrow a Great Eastern Railway single wheeler. In 1868, he designed two types of 2-2-2, both with 7ft 1in driving wheels.

These were key steps in the evolution of the design of the Stirling Single, with the first appearing from Doncaster Works in 1870 followed by another 52.

The first was numbered 1. The GNR did not follow the practice of other lines in having a sequence of numbers for set classes: if a locomotive was scrapped, its number was up for grabs.

Stirling Single No. 1 heads a train of teak coaches at the Doncaster Works open day in 2003. **ROBIN JONES**

Designed especially for high-speed express trains from King's Cross, they cemented the GNR's reputation for speed.

They could haul 275 ton trains at an average speed of 50mph, and lighter trains at 85mph. One of them, No. 775, covered the 82 miles to York in one hour 16 minutes, at an average of 64.7mph.

For many years the Stirling Singles were, as an overall class, the fastest locomotives in England, and indeed the world. Their designer became a living legend among engineers and enthusiasts alike, and the GNR became one of the

most popular routes in the country through his effort.

The GNR never tried to hide the fact that it ran fast expresses. This approach was the opposite of most other British companies of the day, which were mindful of the public corner about high speed and the increased likelihood of crashes.

It was not the only locomotive type that he built for the GNR; there were 2-2-2s for express passenger duties, 2-4-0s and 0-4-2s for branch passenger train and mixed traffic, 0-4-4Ts for suburban passenger trains, 0-6-0s for freight and 0-6-0Ts for shunting.

However, it is the Stirling Single for which he is readily remembered. Its prowess and fleet-footedness were never more underlined than in the two escapades in late Victorian times which came to be known as the Races to the North.

THE RACES TO THE NORTH

The great Victorian age of railway building had left Britain with two major trunk routes from London to Scotland. One was the East Coast Main Line. The other was The West Coast Main Line, comprising the London & North Western Railway and the Caledonian Railway.

LNWR No. 790 *Hardwicke*, the locomotive that produced the highest average speeds in the 1895 Races to the North.

As steam technology developed, so did the intense competition between the operators of both routes, to see who could reach Scotland in the shortest time. The imminent completion of the Forth Bridge gave the fierce rivalry an added incentive.

It may seem incredible today, in this age of health and safety first, but for two summers in the late 19th century, companies actually agreed to race public passenger-carrying trains.

The starting point was London, and the finishing post was Kinnaber Junction, 38 miles south of Aberdeen, where the Caledonian Railway was joined by the North British Railway which, as previously mentioned, had running rights into the granite city. Before Kinnaber Junction, the lines ran on either side of the Montrose Basin, and often trains could see each other as they vied to be the first to get there. This phenomenon was widely reported in press reports at the time.

In late 1887, the East Coast companies decided to allow third-class travel on its 'Flying Scotsman' express. To counter this, the West Coast announced that it would speed up its 10am 'Scotch Express' from June 2, 1888.

A fortnight later, the East Coast responded by announcing that it would be accelerating its services from July 1, 1888.

While the West Coast cut an hour from its 10-hour journey time, the East Coast reduced its nine-hour journey by 30 minutes.

The West Coast responded by also cutting 30 minutes off, and the East Coast again reduced its times by half an hour. Again, it was matched by the West Coast.

The East Coast had thrown off all the shackles, and decided to run its trains as fast as the locomotives could manage.

At first the companies tried to keep their 'races' secret, but as they took place in the summer, and there was little other news around, the press soon got wind of it. The railways were aghast: passengers might just as equally be deterred from travelling by the fear of crashing as encouraged by shorter timings. Indeed, until the press reports appeared, many passengers would have been blissfully unaware that they were taking part in a cutting-edge technology race.

The railways had learned from experience that substantial sections of the travelling public wanted faster trains rather than cheaper fares, and this was especially true on routes such as London to Edinburgh.

On Bank Holiday Monday, August 8, 1888, the West Coast decided to match the East Coast's eight-hour schedule. The rivals maintained this for a week, before

Stirling single 2-2-2 No. 879 – a type that brought cutting-edge speed technology to the ECML in the 19th century. **COLOUR-RAIL**

Stirling Single No. 1: a key stage in the evolution of fast trains along the ECML. **ROBIN JONES**

the East Coast announced that as from August 14, the journey would be cut to seven hours 45 minutes.

The West Coast retaliated by running from London to Edinburgh in seven hours 38 minutes on August 13, with an average speed of 52.3mph.

The next day the rivals met face-to-face and agreed to stop any future accelerations, with the East Coast taking seven hours 45 minutes and the West Coast eight hours.

The accord lasted until August 31 when the East Coast ran as fast as possible to Edinburgh, recording an average speed of 52.7mph.

Overall, the 27 trips involved in the 88 races saw the 105½ miles from King's cross to Grantham covered at an average speed of 55.7mph, taking 113½ minutes. Beyond Grantham, the runs to York were completed at an average speed of 55.5mph.

However, the fastest GNR run was not behind a Stirling Single 4-2-2 but a 2-2-2, which covered the 105 miles from King's Cross to Grantham in 105 minutes.

In September, the races were deemed to be over, and both sides reverted to the July timetables, the East Coast taking eight hours 15 minutes and the West Coast eight hours and 30 minutes.

At a time when railway companies were extolling the virtues of train travel for business and leisure, the publicity generated by the races probably did them nothing but good.

The second Race to the North took place in 1895, and again the Stirling Singles played a starring role. It may be deemed to have begun when the East Coast decided to speed up the 8pm service from King's Cross on July 1, cutting 15 minutes off the schedule. At the same time coincidentally or otherwise, the West Coast announced it was cutting 10 minutes off its 8pm service. Small beer.

However, on July 14, the West Coast announced that it would cut the London to

Hardwicke hauls a rake of three coaches from the during the Rainhill 150 event in 1980.
BRIAN SHARPE

Aberdeen journey time to 11 hours, by losing 40 minutes, and launched a mass publicity campaign. Eight days later, the East Coast announced it was speeding up its 8pm Aberdeen express, by cutting off 15 minutes to reduce the journey time to 10 hours 45 minutes, so it would arrive at 6.35pm, 10 minutes sooner than the rival train.

However, the first few days of racing saw the West Coast trains arrive even earlier, beating their rivals on most occasions.

On August 20, the Great Northern Railway's Stirling Single 4-2-2 No. 668 took the East Coast express 105½ miles from King's Cross to Grantham in just one hour 41 minutes with an average speed of 62.7mph. An engine change saw No. 775 take over, and complete the 82 miles to York in one hour 16 minutes, an average speed of 64.7mph.

The overall 393 mile trip was covered in six hours 19 minutes, at a speed of 63.5 mph, while the extended run to Aberdeen, making a total of 523 miles, took eight hours 40 minutes, with an average speed 60.4 mph.

On the night of August 21-22, the East Coast's 8pm express arrived at Aberdeen at 4.40am, setting a new record. After that, the East Coast stopped its racing.

The LNWR responded the next day, and a storming run by Improved Precedent or 'Jumbo' express passenger 2-4-0 No. 790 *Hardwicke* took two hours and six minutes to cover the 141 miles from Crewe to Carlisle with an average speed of 67.1 mph, setting a new speed record in the Races to the North.

Records showed that the North Eastern Railway produced the highest average speeds on the East Coast route, when Gateshead-based driver Bob Nicholson and his fireman Tom Blades took Wordsdell M1 4-4-0 No. 1620 to an average speed of 81mph over the 2.7 miles between Cocksburnpath and Innerwick. The pair covered the 75 miles from Longhirst to Dunbar driving No. 1620 at an average speed of 67.3mph.

Only *Hardwicke*, now preserved in the National Railway Museum at York, achieved higher long-distance average speeds than this. On August 22-23, No. 790 ran the 8.2 miles between Plumpton and Wreay at an average of 82mph, and covered the 73.4 miles from Minshull Vernon to Carnforth at an average of 68.3mph.

The best East Coast average was the Great Northern's 74.2mph over the 12.2 miles Between Hitchin and Sandy.

Observers felt that the West Coast had the edge in the six weeks of racing, although there was never deemed an overall winner.

However, the railway companies were brought sharply down to earth on July 13, 1896 with a serious derailment on a tight curve at Preston, when a Euston to Glasgow train passed through the station at around 45mph, ignoring the 10mph (16 km/h) speed limit and leaving one person dead.

GNR No. 1 in passenger service again during its visit to the Great Central Railway in 1981/82.
BRIAN SHARPE

This incident led to public demands for an end to staged train racing and more emphasis placed on safety.

Also, passengers on the racing trains found that they were arriving at Aberdeen much earlier than the scheduled breakfast time of 7am and had to wait on the empty station before connecting trains could arrive. So the rivals reached a fresh agreement on speed limits.

Furthermore, Stirling Singles were involved in two serious accidents on the ECML itself around this time. In the first, at St Neots on November 10, 1896, No. 1006 was hauling the night 'Scotch Express' when a rail broke as the engine passed over at 60mph. The last four out of nine coaches became separated from the train and crashed into loaded coal wagons in a siding.

Four months later, a second accident involving trackwork, this time at Little Bytham on Stoke Bank, saw an Up 'Leeds Diner' hauled by No. 1003 at 70mph at a section where not only had ballasting not been completed, but the flagman whose job it was to provide warning had been removed.

The unballasted track became distorted by the engine movement and several carriages at the rear became detached, one hitting a bridge parapet and dividing from its underframe, killing three passengers, with another carriage running down the embankment into a field.

Such was the public fear of trains running at too high a speed that when the Great Western Railway's No. 3440 *City of Truro* allegedly became the first in the world to break the 100mph barrier, touching 102.3mph with the 'Ocean Mails' on Wellington Bank in Somerset in May 1904, the company kept quiet about it for many years.

And it was only in the December 1907 edition of *The Railway Magazine* nearly four years later that the alleged speed appeared

The great 8ft single driving wheels of the Stirling Singles gave them a huge advantage over contemporary locomotives. **ROBIN JONES**

GNR No. 1 is towed along the main line by LNER A4 Pacific No. 4498 *Sir Nigel Gresley*. **BRIAN SHARPE**

publicly for the first time, and even then was not attributed to a particular engine. Readers had to wait until the following April's edition for its identity to be revealed.

Truro's feat came nearly five years after a series of high-speed test runs took place on the Lancashire & Yorkshire Railway's Liverpool Exchange-Southport line using locomotives from Aspinall's newly-introduced 'High Flyer' 4-4-2 class. On July 15, 1899 one such train was formed of Southport-based No. 1392 and five coaches. Timed to leave Liverpool Exchange at 2.51pm, it was allegedly recorded as passing milepost 17 in 12.75mins.

This gives a start-to-pass speed of 80mph but, given the permanent 20mph restriction at Bank Hall and the 65mph restriction at Waterloo, the suggestion has been made that this train attained 100mph.

The L&Y never published details or timings of this test run. It is only because the passing times were 'unofficially' noted by local enthusiasts that this obscure 100mph claim is known at all.

After the Preston calamity, the old East and West Coast rivalries were suppressed, for several decades as it happened. But they never went away.

A LNWR apprentice under Francis Webb at the time of the Races to the North was none other than young Herbert Nigel Gresley.

THE ABBOTS RIPTON CRASH

A train crash on the ECML in 1876 had far reaching consequences for the whole network, for it changed British railway signalling practice.

The Abbots Ripton rail disaster occurred on January 21, 1876 at Abbots Ripton, then a station 4½ miles to the north of Huntingdon.

Up till then, the GNR main line had a safety record second to none.

However, during a blizzard, the 'Special Scotch Express' running from Edinburgh to London collided with a coal train at speed.

The coal train was running in front of the 'Express' and was scheduled to be shunted into a siding at Abbots Ripton to allow the faster train to pass.

The snowstorm had delayed both trains and so the signalman at Holme, the station north of Abbots Ripton, decided to allow the coal train into sidings there to allow the 'Express' to pass, and set his signals accordingly.

The coal train ignored the signals, or could not see them, and carried on towards Abbots Ripton where the scheduled shunting movement took place. That had all but been achieved when the 'Express' ran into it at speed. Several wagons were smashed, but the coal train locomotive escaped serious damage. The express engine derailed and ended up lying on its side, leaving its tender and two carriages blocking the down line.

The 'Express' crew walked back up the up line towards Wood Walton, laying detonators on the rails to warn any further trains to stop.

The coal train engine ran light to Huntingdon to seek assistance, while the shocked signalman repeatedly tried to use the speaking telegraph to contact

Huntingdon station, but the signalmen there did not answer at first. When he finally did, he took a jobsworth approach by refusing to accept any message which did not start with a code indicating the time it was sent, and then responded by indicating he was busy.

He was handling the passage of a 13-coach express train running in the opposite direction to Leeds – which hit the wreckage minutes later.

It was found that the original cause of the crash was placing too much reliance on signals and block working that allowed high-speed running even when the conditions were not up to it.

The follow-on crash was deemed to have been caused by the inadequate braking performance of the second express and its crew's failure to implement emergency procedures promptly and correctly.

The GNR was using the block system which everyone believed would prevent such accidents. Accordingly, the details of the accident greatly alarmed other railway companies that relied on it.

The railway also used lower quadrant semaphore signals. It was found that the weight of snow on the semaphore arm and snow and ice on the wires by which the arm was moved prevented the signals from showing danger, after signalmen had pulled the levers. While this would not have been so great a problem on a clear day, in snowstorms, signalmen could not see their signals.

AT A TIME WHEN RAILWAY COMPANIES WERE EXTOLLING THE VIRTUES OF TRAIN TRAVEL FOR BUSINESS AND LEISURE, THE PUBLICITY GENERATED BY THE RACES PROBABLY DID THEM NOTHING BUT GOOD.

A contemporary sketch of the scene of the Abbots Ripton train crash. **ILLUSTRATED LONDON NEWS**

Accordingly, the 'Express' had passed a series of signals which had been set to danger but were showing clear.

Therefore, it may be deemed as an accident waiting to happen.

A total of 13 passengers died and 53 others and six train crew members were injured.

A Court of Inquiry reported on February 23 and rejected the conclusion of the coroner's jury that the block system was at fault and had proved ineffective in a case of emergency. The problem lay with signals.

The court criticised the Holme stationmaster for not stopping the 'Express', the Wood Walton signalman for not using detonators or a handlamp to stop the same train and the delay of the signalman at Huntingdon in answering Abbots Ripton.

The inquiry report recommended that signals were improved so that they worked correctly in frost and snow, and that they gave an indication to the signalman if they are not operating properly

Also, it recommended that signals should not normally be set as clear, but at danger, so

An East Coast Class 125 unit passes the site of Kinnaber Junction today. The Brechin to Kinnaber Junction line closed to all traffic in 1981 and the junction is now lifted and overgrown. **KH TULYAR/CREATIVE COMMONS**

Heroic *Hardwicke* may have won the day for the West Coast route to Scotland in the eyes of many observers, but it now has a permanent home next to the East Coast Main Line, in the form of the National Railway Museum in York. **ROBIN JONES**

that if they stick in bad weather, they would not wrongly show clear.

Noting that the Leeds express did not have continuous braking, it called for improvement of braking systems on trains.

The GNR responded by changing to a new type of semaphore in the form of the 'somersault' signal.

The main feature of the type was the pivot about which the arm moved was at the middle of the arm, so that accumulation of snow should not significantly affect its balance.

The modern practice of the 'normal' position for signals being 'danger' was adopted everywhere.

Furthermore, railway companies were required by law to inform the Board of Trade each year about how much of the carriage stock had continuous brakes. Further accidents elsewhere led to continuous braking on passenger trains becoming mandatory.

Abbots Ripton lost its passenger services on September 15, 1968 as part of a rationalisation of village stations on the ECML. Goods facilities were withdrawn in 1964, and now there is no station between Huntingdon and Peterborough.

No. 1

Stirling Single No. 1 is now part of the National Collection and displayed at Locomotion: The National Railway Museum in Shildon.

When it was withdrawn from traffic in 1907, it was preserved, first at King's Cross shed after being displayed at an exhibition in Wembley in 1909, and then at Doncaster Works. In 1925, the LNER gave it a new boiler so it could star in the 1925 Stockton & Darlington Railway centenary cavalcade, and the following year, entered a new railway museum set up at York by the LNER.

In 1938, the LNER resteamed it to haul a 'Scotsman' train of the 1870s comprising seven East Coast Joint Stock six-wheelers as part of publicity surrounding the introduction of new streamlined trains. The Railway Correspondence & Travel Society also hired it for a main line railtour. It became the first preserved engine to do so. In the early Eighties, it returned to steam, and briefly ran on the Great Central Railway and the North Yorkshire Moors Railway.

In 2010, it starred in a critically-acclaimed stage production of Edith A Nesbit's classic *The Railway Children* at the redundant Waterloo International platform. Shunted into position during the performances by a Class 08 diesel, a fog machine was used to generate the smoke effects.

In 1898, an 18in gauge model of No. 1 was built by students at London's Regent Street Polytechnic. They included Henry Greenly who found fame as a builder of similar miniature locomotives for lines like the Romney, Hythe & Dymchurch Railway.

The scaled-down Stirling single was sold to E F S Notter, who was the GNR's district locomotive superintendent based at King's Cross, and who later kept it in King's Cross Shed, home of the full-size originals. After changing hands several times, the locomotive is now at the World of Country Life Museum at Sandy Bay, Exmouth. ∎

The Atlantic era

With the development of dining facilities on board, both for first and third-class passengers, and with the Races to the North finished, the emphasis on the Great Northern Railway switched from speed to amenities.

The GNR soon found it would not have it all its own way linking Manchester to London via Nottingham and the ECML. The Manchester, Sheffield & Lincolnshire Railway completed its London Extension to Marylebone in 1899, turning itself into the Great Central Railway.

The GNR managed to keep its King's Cross to Manchester expresses, while at the same time the demand for freight expanded. The company found itself needing another 70 engines at the end of the Victorian era.

Stirling's successor was Henry Alfred Ivatt, whose railway career had begun at the age of 17 when he was apprenticed to John Ramsbottom at the LNWR's Crewe Works. He eventually rose to become head of the Chester District before taking up a post with Ireland's Great Southern & Western Railway in 1877. He became its locomotive superintendent for the Southern District.

In 1895, he became locomotive superintendent of the GNR.

Recalling the accidents which befell the Stirling Singles because of poor track, Ivatt walked the whole 156 mile length of the GNR and was appalled at the condition of the permanent way.

He rebuilt the Stirling Singles with larger boilers and cylinders. He eventually went on to produce a new class of singles – the last to be made. They had similar front ends to the Stirling singles, and shared their driving wheel size. They were classified as A4s and all were withdrawn in 1917.

Ivatt introduced the first Atlantic locomotives to Britain. The name Atlantic, used to refer to a 4-4-2 wheel arrangement, may have originated from the use of such locomotives on the 70mph express trains of the US's Atlantic Coast Line in 1895.

He was also the first to introduce Walschaerts valve gear to this country.

Invented by Belgian railway mechanical engineer Egide Walschaerts in 1844, it offered the advantage that it could be mounted entirely on the outside of a locomotive, leaving the space between the frames clear. Whereas Stephenson valve gear remained the most commonly-used valve gear on 19th-century locomotives, the Walschaerts valve gear took precedence in the 20th century.

Under Ivatt, big boilers, not massive single driving wheels and faster running, were the trend. His first engines were 4-4-0s carrying some of the biggest boilers in Britain, but for him, they were not big enough. He extended the locomotive frames and added a pair of carrying wheels so he could make the boilers even bigger, increasing their length from 10ft 1in to 13ft.

In doing so, he produced his first Atlantic, No. 990, in 1898. It was the first of a class known as Klondikes in 1898.

In December 1902, he built No. 251, the first of his Large Atlantics, by adapting the design and increasing the boiler diameter from 4ft 8in to 5ft 6in.

Grantham-based Ivatt Atlantic No. 1415, later 4415, on the turntable at Doncaster Works. **JOHN CRAWLEY COLLECTION**

The GNR classified both types as C1, but the LNER classified the large boiler variation as C1 and the small boiler variation as C2.

The Atlantics all had tiny cylinders, and therefore their tractive effort was less than that of the Stirling Singles. However, they had better adhesion because of the extra driving wheels, and the larger boiler could hold steaming rates for longer. The need has switched from fast trains to pulling bigger and heavier ones.

So the Atlantics superseded the Stirling Singles, which were relegated to very much secondary routes for a few years before all but No. 1 were withdrawn and scrapped.

Ivatt worked on developing his Atlantics, producing several different types, and modifying existing ones. His last development was the fitting of piston valves and Schmidt 18-row superheaters to the last 10 C1s that were built in 1910, not to increase power, but so he could reduce the boiler pressure and maintenance costs.

Ivatt's successor Nigel Gresley added 24-element superheaters from 1912 and raised the boiler pressure, and later fitted 32-element superheaters. As such, Ivatt's Atlantics continued to be used on top-link duties throughout the Thirties, including the Pullman trains from King's Cross.

The C1s experienced a high degree of development, resulting in five different cylinder arrangements, and four different superheater arrangements, during their time with the LNER, but Gresley chose to build no more Atlantics.

While there may have been a lull in speed a record attempts, the C1s could still show their mettle. In July 1936, after a Gresley A3 failed at Grantham, it was replaced by the station pilot, C1 No. 4404. It reached Selby in 67 minutes and 41 seconds, covering more than 60 miles at an average of 64mph.

Only two Ivatt Atlantics survived into British Railways' day, the last, No. 62822, withdrawn in November 250. No. 251 was taken out of traffic in 1947 and preserved. In 1953 it was steamed for a series of specials celebrating the centenary of Doncaster Works, and again the following year.

It is now part of the National Collection, on display at Bressingham Steam Museum in Norfolk.

Ivatt's son George Ivatt became the post-war chief mechanical engineer of the LMS, while his daughter Marjorie married Oliver Bulleid, CME of the Southern Railway, famous for his streamlined Pacifics. Henry Ivatt died in 1923 in Sussex.

The two preserved Ivatt Atlantics took part in a special run to mark the centenary of Doncaster works on September 20, 1953. Two of the greatest ECML drivers of the day took part: Bill Hoole was the driver on No. 251, which together with No. 990 Henry Oakley, hauled the 'Plant Centenarian' from King's Cross to Doncaster, while Ted Hailstone drove No. 60014 *Silver Link*, which took it back to London, incidentally hitting 96mph on Stoke Bank and covering the journey in 147 minutes seven seconds non-stop. **BOB JOHNSON**

Pioneer Ivatt Atlantic No. 251 at Bressingham in Norfolk. **BRIAN SHARPE**

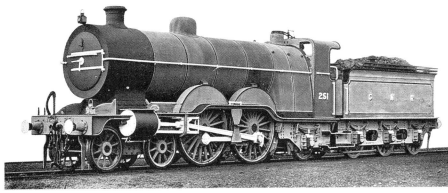

No. 251 pictured in 1907 in GNR livery. **ROBIN JONES COLLECTION**

NORTH EASTERN ATLANTICS

Ivatt's Atlantics were not the only ones running on the ECML.

Vincent Raven, chief mechanical engineer of the North Eastern Railway from 1910-22, produced his 4-4-2s in response to the company's demand for increased speed.

Raven, an advocate of three-cylinder locomotives, in August 1910 was given the green light to build the first 12 C7 Atlantics, later Class Z under the LNER.

The first 20 were built the following year by the North British Locomotive Company. There were 10 built with saturated boilers and the others with superheated boilers, allowing a direct comparison. Superheating was quickly found to be superior, and it was adopted for all

At first, the C7s were used on express passenger services. From 1924, C7s ran through to King's Cross hauling specials to the British Empire Exhibition, and specials for football finals, also at Wembley.

Raven developed the design into a Pacific, to counter the Great Northern Railway's announcement that it was building a 4-6-2, as seen in the next chapter. He stretched the C7 design by increasing the boiler diameter and cylinder size. Boiler pressure was increased from 175psi to 200psi.

Greater power and acceleration was urgently needed for the increasing loads

on the ECML, and the NER authorised the building of the first two at Darlington Works on March 30, 1922. Numbered 2400 and 2401, they were both delivered in December 1922 just before the Grouping.

The A2 was the biggest locomotive the NER built, but it was not regarded as its best. For their first 10 years, the A2s were used between and Grantham and Edinburgh, with some runs to Leeds, primarily handling heavy secondary express passenger trains on the ECML. Their limited route availability combined with the need for new boilers led to them being superseded by Gresley's V2 2-6-2s, and withdrawn between 1936-37. Indeed, No. 2402 has the dubious distinction of being the first locomotive built by the LNER to be scrapped. The Class Zs were all were scrapped by the early Fifties.

RAVEN'S ELECTRIC PLANS

Raven himself had his own views as to the future direction of the ECML and its express trains. In short, he wanted to see the route electrified, and had been designing a 4-6-4 electric locomotive to pay the way.

He had begun his career with the NER in 1877 under locomotive superintendent Edward Fletcher and by 1893 he had become assistant mechanical engineer to Wilson Worsdell. He was delegated to work on the

NER three-cylinder Atlantic No. 728 departing from Newcastle with the Up Waverley-King's Cross express. **RJ PURVIS**

King's Cross-based Ivatt C1 Atlantic No. 3279 heads a Down stopping train at Potter's Bar in 1934. Built in 1907 as a two-cylinder locomotive, Gresley had it rebuilt in 1915 as a four-cylinder simple engine with outside Walschaerts value gear. The locomotive was withdrawn in 1948. **JOHN CRAWLEY COLLECTION**

NER's pioneering North Tyneside suburban route electrification, involving a 600 volts DC third rail system.

In 1915, a section of the NER between Shildon and Newport on Teesside was electrified with 1500V DC overhead pick-up in a bid to improve coal trains. The 10 centre cab 1100hp electric locomotives were built at Darlington Works.

The scheme was deemed a success, so much so that Raven began drawing up plans to similarly electrify the ECML from York to Newcastle.

The blueprint went as far as having a prototype passenger locomotive constructed at Darlington in 1922. NER No. 13 had a 4-6-4 wheel arrangement and 1800hpo, and was successfully trialled on the Shildon-Newport route.

However, the Grouping of 1923 saw the electrification plan scrapped, and steam still reigning supreme on the ECML. Indeed, steam returned to the Shildon-Newport route when its electrification was scrapped in 1935.

What if history taken a different course, and Raven's electric line, not Nigel Gresley's later Pacifics, had become the order of the day on the ECML in the Twenties, rather than having to wait another six decades? ■

Sir Henry Oakley became general manager of the GNR in 1870, and also served as secretary of the Railway Companies' Association. He was knighted in 1891 and in June 1900, a C1 Atlantic, No. 990, was named after him, two years after he retired. It was preserved following withdrawal in 1937 and can now be seen at Bressingham Steam Museum in Norfolk. After leaving the GNR he became chairman of the Central London Railway, one of the new underground lines and died in February 1912, aged 88. The locomotive is pictured during a heritage era visit to Boston in Lincolnshire. **BRIAN SHARPE**

CHAPTER EIGHT

The summit of world speed

A4 No. 4468 *Mallard* passes Potters Bar in July 1938. **COLOUR-RAIL**

Sir Nigel Gresley meets *Sir Nigel Gresley,* his 100th Pacific locomotive. **THE RAILWAY MAGAZINE**

The Races to the North were, in retrospect, a trial run. The best was yet to come, not only for the East Coast Main Line, but world steam railway technology.

The 1930s were to be the zenith of the steam age. It was the great decade when, before the clouds of war appeared on the horizon, the steam locomotive concept was taken to dizzy new heights that back in Victorian times few would have imagined possible.

Speed record after record was broken as the East and West Coast lines tore up their 1896 agreement to stop racing, and once again, it was the sky's the limit on the great run from London to Scotland.

On the West Coast, the LMS had Swindon-trained chief mechanical engineer Sir William Stanier. Facing him, almost as if in a boxing ring, was the East Coast's Nigel Gresley.

The competition between the pair to produce the best and most powerful locomotives pushed the transport technology of the day to its utmost limits and a few miles beyond.

Most importantly, Britain – the country that had invented the steam locomotive – was left standing head and shoulders above the rest of the world in the transport sector. In the aftermath of the Second World War, would we ever feel the same way about our railways?

BORN IN EDINBURGH

Herbert Nigel Gresley was born on June 19, 1876 in Edinburgh. His parents were English: his father was the Reverend Nigel Gresley, rector of St Peter's church in Netherseal, Derbyshire, and his mother had visited the Scottish capital to see a gynaecologist.

The Gresley family had roots in Derbyshire dating back many centuries.

Young Nigel attended a preparatory school in St Leonards, Sussex, and then Marlborough College in Wiltshire, where he developed his abilities for mechanical drawing and was top of the form in science.

After school he joined the London & North Western Railway under locomotive superintendent Francis Webb, the 'King of Crewe', as an apprentice. He then moved to the Lancashire & Yorkshire Railway works at Horwich, at the time overseen by senior engineer Sir John Aspinall. His engineering skills earned him swift promotion.

He married his wife, Ethel Frances Fullagar, in 1901, and three years later became assistant superintendent of the carriage and wagon department of the L&YR.

In 1905, the couple moved from Newton Heath in Manchester with their first two children to Doncaster where, at the age of 29, he took up the post of carriage and wagon superintendent with the Great Northern Railway. When in 1911 Henry A Ivatt retired as locomotive superintendent, Gresley he was given the job.

Neither the ECML nor steam would ever be the same again.

During the First World War he oversaw the production of munitions at Doncaster Works, became a Lieutenant-Colonel in the Engineer and Railway Staff Corps, RE(TF), and was awarded a CBE in January 1920.

At the Grouping of 1923, Gresley took over the role of LNER chief mechanical engineer and moved to King's Cross. The Gresleys had two more children.

His wife died in August 1929, and afterwards he spent time in Canada with his eldest daughter. While he was there, he drove one of the Canadian Pacific locomotives in British Columbia.

After returning home, he eventually bought Salisbury Hall, an Elizabethan house near St Albans which had a moat in which he built up a collection of several species of wild duck as pets… including mallards.

He was knighted in 1936 during the brief reign of Edward VIII, and that same year he was awarded an honorary doctorate of science by Manchester University.

> **SPEED RECORD AFTER RECORD WAS BROKEN AS THE EAST AND WEST COAST LINES TORE UP THEIR 1896 AGREEMENT TO STOP RACING**

Sir Nigel Gresley: was he the greatest steam locomotive designer of them all?

THE FIRST BRITISH PACIFIC

The first 4-6-2 or 'Pacific' steam locomotive built in Britain was also the only one that the Great Western Railway ever constructed.

No. 111 *The Great Bear* was produced by George Jackson Churchward at Swindon Works in February 1908.

Nobody knows for certain why it was built; it may be that the GWR board wanted the company to gain the prestige of building the first British Pacific, as well as the biggest and heaviest engine of the day.

The 4-6-2s were named Pacifics after, it was believed, locomotives supplied in 1902 by the United States manufacturer Baldwin for the Missouri Pacific Railroad.

Another explanation is that following his development of the GWR 4-6-0s, Churchward wanted to prove that his designs were also sound when it came to larger locomotive boilers.

The Great Bear proved that it was possible to build a four-cylinder locomotive with 15in diameter cylinders which could be sufficiently fed by a standard GWR boiler.

However, its sheer size led to *The Great Bear* being restricted to the Paddington to Bristol line because of its high axle loading which gave it a route availability of 'Special Red', although on one occasion it was recorded as having run to Wolverhampton.

The Great Bear experienced early problems with clearance on curves and springing of the trailing wheels. Modifications were also made to the

superheating of the boiler.

In January 1924 *The Great Bear*, needing heavy repairs to its boiler after just 527,272 miles, was dismantled and the parts used to build one of Charles Collett's Castle class 4-6-0s. Churchward, who had by then retired, was disappointed.

He had earlier heard that Gresley was planning to build a Pacific for the GNR and said: "What did that young man want to build it for? We could have sold him ours!"

The locomotive that had been *The Great Bear* kept its number, but was renamed *Viscount Churchill*, and with an expanded route availability, remained in traffic until withdrawal in 1953 and scrapped.

The pioneer Gresley A1 Pacific No. 4470 *Great Northern* emerges from Wood Green tunnel on a down express, c1930. The first 11 A1s were built to the more generous Great Northern loading gauge with a taller chimney, dome and cab. No. 4470 was cut down to the composite LNER loading gauge in May 1933. Also shown is a somersault distant signal on 'gallows' type brackets. **NRM**

GRESLEY'S FIRST PACIFICS

Gresley was indeed planning to build two Pacifics for services on the ECML. Two were built at Doncaster by the GNR before the Grouping, the first, No. 1470 *Great Northern*, being named after the company. It was the first of a class intended to handle express trains that were becoming too big for Ivatt's large-boilered Atlantics.

It was Ivatt's Atlantics that began the GNR's big engine policy. His C1 class was designed as a powerful free-steaming locomotive capable of heading the GNR's fastest and heaviest express trains, sometimes weighing more than 500 tons. The first of them, No. 251, appeared in 1902, with 80 more built at Doncaster between 1904-8.

In 1915, Gresley drew up plans for a longer version of the Ivatt Atlantic but with

LNER driver J Burfoot, who joined the GNR as a cleaner in 1895 and in 1913 qualified as a driver, later workedT on several express trains including the 'Coronation' and 'Silver Jubilee.' He retired in 1943. **THE RAILWAY MAGAZINE**

four cylinders, but he found his design to be unsatisfactory. He then looked at the Pennsylvania Railroad's new K4 Pacific, the final evolution of a series of prototypes produced in 1910/11, and which were so successful that they remained as that line's main passenger locomotive until the end of steam in 1957. The K4 is recognised as the State Steam Locomotive of Pennsylvania.

Gresley eagerly devoured the technical reports of the K4 and its immediate predecessors, and they gave him the insight to design a modern steam locomotive for Britain.

His Pacifics exploited the maximum limits of the ECML loading gauge with large boilers and wide fireboxes providing a large grate area. The firebox followed GNR tradition in being a round-topped version, not the flat-topped Belpaire type on the K4s. Heat transfer and the flow of gases were aided by a combustion chamber which extended forward from the firebox space into the boiler barrel,

Gresley's universal three-cylinder layout was again a feature of his A1s, after being incorporated into two of his earlier designs.

After the first two Pacifics appeared in 1922, the other being No. 1471 *Sir Frederick Banbury*, the GNR ordered 10 more. They were being built when the LNER took over.

Gresley's GNR Pacific type became the standard LNER express passenger locomotive and was designated Class A1. A total of 31 were built at Doncaster and another 20 contracted out to the North British Locomotive Company.

One flaw was that Gresley's first Pacifics had been designed to work on the GNR, which involved distances of no more than 200 miles. With the formation of the LNER, and the three East Coast companies coming under one umbrella, they had to work greater distances.

A1 No. 1472, which had been outshopped in the early days of the LNER yet first given a GNR number, was renumbered 4472 and

named *Flying Scotsman* for display at the British Empire Exhibition at Wembley along with the GWR's first Castle 4-6-0, No. 4073 *Caerphilly Castle*, which the Swindon empire boasted was the most powerful locomotive in Britain with a tractive effort of 31,825lb.

In the two months following the exhibition, the LNER and GWR ran exchange trials to establish just which had produced a superior locomotive. *Pendennis Castle* won the day for the GWR, climbing the ECML from King's Cross to Finsbury Park in less than six minutes, which the Pacifics could not match, and with greater coal and water economy. The following year it was *Pendennis Castle* that was exhibited at the second British Empire Exhibition, alongside *Flying Scotsman*, and with a notice boasting that it was Britain's most powerful locomotive.

Undaunted, Gresley learned much from the trials. In 1926, a series of experimental modifications were made to A1 No. 4477 *Gay Crusader*, based on Swindon practice.

The valve gear was adjusted to both boost the performance of the Pacifics with their 180psi boilers while using less coal and water, making long-distance non-stop runs a possibility.

The valve gear was subsequently fitted to No. 2555 *Centenary* in 1927, and the rest of the class followed suit over a period of several years.

Meanwhile, a new A3 class of Pacific appeared, taking on board the tests and improvements made to the A1s. The first was No. 2743 *Felstead* which was outshopped in August 1928 with a 220psi boiler, increased superheat and improved weight distribution.

Another new feature was the change from right to left-hand drive, making it easier to sight signals.

A total of 27 A3s were built from new, and eventually all of the original A1s, including *Flying Scotsman*, were converted to A3s. The last A1 to be converted was No. 60068 *Sir Visto* in 1949.

Under wraps: *Flying Scotsman* concealed from public view as it is delivered to the British Empire Exhibition at Wembley in 1924. **NRM**

Flying Scotsman seen leaving Leeds station with the 'White Rose' express for King's Cross in 1956. The photographer, Bishop Eric Treacy, was often allowed special access to many areas denied to other railway photographers. He also befriended many of the footplate crews, occasionally persuading them to create special smoke effects for the camera. **NRM**

No. 4472 *Flying Scotsman* at
King's Cross on July 24, 1933.
CCB HERBERT/NRM

THE NEW KINGS OF SPEED

Gresley's A1 Pacifics immediately showed that they could handle bigger loads at faster speeds than the Ivatt Atlantics. During a test run, No. 1470 *Great Northern* hauled a 20-coach 600 ton train over the 105 miles from London to Grantham while recording average speed of 51.8mph, but burned a huge amount of coal in the process.

However, the huge benefits of the subsequent modifications to the design became apparent with the launch of the daily 'Flying Scotsman' named train (see separate chapter) from King's Cross to Edinburgh in 1928, first hauled by a pool of three A1s and two A3s, including *Flying Scotsman* with its modified valve gear, and which hauled the first train on May 1, 1928. The following year, No. 4472 starred in the film The *Flying Scotsman*, which was set aboard the train of the same name and featured several daring stunts performed while it was in motion.

However, No. 4472's greatest claim to fame came on November 30, 1934.

While hauling a light test train between London and Leeds, the return trip with six coaches weighing 208 tons saw No. 4472 reach 100mph just outside Little Bytham on Stoke Bank. It held the speed for another 600 yards.

The driver, William Sparshatt, then 61, had remarked to onlookers before he left King's Cross that day: "If we hit anything today, we'll hit it hard."

The Down trip to Leeds had been completed in 152 minutes for the 185½ miles. It would be another three decades before a similar timing was achieved on King's Cross-Leeds.

There was no secrecy of the type that surrounded *City of Truro's* alleged 102.3mph feat in 1904. The rivalry with the West Coast route was now back on big time, and the LNER publicity machine could not wait to make the most of *Flying Scotsman's* achievement in Lincolnshire.

City of Truro probably did 100mph before, but *Flying Scotsman's* achievement was the first time that it was officially recorded.

THE 'FLYING HAMBURGER'

The resumption of the race to cut timings on the ECML came about because of developments in the German Reich, namely, the appearance of the 'Flying Hamburger', a streamlined two-car diesel electric railcar set which quickly became the fastest train in the world, and if not sounding a death knell for steam, then giving a loud warning of one.

State railway Deutsche Reichsbahn-Gesellschaft ordered the 98-seater Class SVT 877 set in 1932 from manufacturer Waggon und Maschinenbau AG Gorlitz and it entered service on the Berlin-Hamburg line the following year.

Wind tunnel experiments were used to design the streamlining, following on from the development of the high-speed inter-urban railcar Bullet two years previously. Each of the two vehicles had a 12-cylinder Maybach diesel engine with a direct current generator directly coupled to it, which drove a Tatzlager-traction motor.

The 'Flying Hamburger' reached the then-astounding average speed of 77.4mph over the 178 mile journey, decades ahead of its time. It became the prototype for the DRG Class SVT 137 units.

The 'Flying Hamburger' showed that diesel propulsion would sooner or later become a new stage in railway development. However, steam at that time was still more cost effective, and locomotive designers looked in depth at ways in which the aerodynamic advantages of streamlining could also be applied to steam trains.

German locomotive builder Henschel-Werke subsequently produced an express steam train that could compete with the likes of the Flying Hamburger. The Henschel-Wegmann Train ran non-stop express services between Berlin and Dresden from June 1936 to August 1939. Two Class 61 steam locomotives were built to haul it, one a 4-6-4T and the other a 4-6-2T. Both the locomotives and the coaches were streamlined.

In the US, high-speed diesel railcars were introduced on the Union Pacific Railroad and Burlington Railroad with resounding success. The LNER watched with great interest and decided that it too wanted a train that could match the Flying Hamburger in terms of speed.

Gresley rode on the German train and was so impressed that the LNER seriously considered buying one.

The manufacturer was asked to design a Flying Hamburger for the LNER. However, it could not promise a higher average speed than 63mph between London and Newcastle, 14mph less than the German railcar. The problem was due to the heavier gradients and speed restrictions of the ECML.

Furthermore, the passenger accommodation was cramped, and hardly likely to attract passengers used to the spacious comfort of standard East Coast rolling stock.

The chief general manager of the LNER, Sir Ralph Wedgwood, suggested that with an ordinary Pacific engine, faster overall speeds could be maintained with a train of much greater weight, capacity, and comfort.

This was the way the company chose to go. In March 1935, A3 No. 2750 turned in a series of outstanding performances on the ECML. Running from King's Cross to Newcastle and back, *Papyrus* reached 108mph going down Stoke Bank while hauling 217 tons. It maintained a speed above 100mph for 12½ consecutive miles, the world record for a non-streamlined locomotive, shared with a French Chapelon Pacific.

Papyrus showed that it might even have been possible to work a four-hour service between King's Cross and Newcastle using A3 Pacifics, with a load of 200-220 tons.

CITY OF TRURO **PROBABLY DID 100MPH BEFORE, BUT** *FLYING SCOTSMAN'S* **ACHIEVEMENT WAS THE FIRST TIME THAT IT WAS OFFICIALLY RECORDED.**

A3 Pacific No. 2751 *Humorist* fitted with a Kylchap blastpipe and smoke-deflecting plates. The LNER had a policy of naming most of its A1s and A3s after racehorses, *Flying Scotsman* being one of five exceptions.
OS NOCK/THE RAILWAY MAGAZINE

STREAMLINING WINS THE DAY

Streamlining, however, was by this stage being seen as the way forward.

The aim was not only to reduce air resistance at high speed, but also for publicity purposes, to boost the glamour appeal of big express steam locomotives.

At first, modifications to the front ends of existing LNER Pacifics were considered. Experiments were conducted using scale models at the National Physical Laboratory to determine a shape that would both reduce air resistance and lift the exhaust steam effectively at high speed. It was shown that streamlining an A3 could save more than 40hp at 60mph rising to 97 at 80mph and 138hp at 90mph. Overall, a saving in power output of about 10% could be made, it was shown, and these findings were later confirmed by full-size engines in service.

Following the success of the *Papyrus* trials, Gresley was given the go-ahead to build the 'Silver Jubilee' streamlined trains.

Not only were the locomotives streamlined but the coaches were too, painted silver with valences between the bogies and flexible covers over the coach ends.

The seven-coach train could carry 198 passengers and comprised a twin-articulated brake third carriage, triple-articulated restaurant set and a twin-articulated first class carriage.

The locomotive, designated an A4, had art-deco wedge-shaped streamlining that had been inspired by a Bugatti railcar which Gresley saw in France.

The design was refined with the assistance of Professor W E Dalby and the wind tunnel facilities at the National Physical Laboratory at Teddington.

One key area as far as these tests were concerned was the lifting of smoke away from the cab. The design achieved this without deflectors. An important feature here is the slight depression immediately behind the chimney, without which it was found that, in a side wind, the eddy currents on the leeward side of the engine caused quite serious obscuring of the driver's outlook.

The first of the new Pacifics was No. 2509 *Silver Link*. Immediately it raised eyebrows,

A4 No. 2509 *Silver Link* passes Potters Bar on its inaugural run with the 'Silver Jubilee' on September 27, 1935. **ER WETHERSETT/THE RAILWAY MAGAZINE**

and destroyed anyone's notion of what a steam locomotive should look like. Observers either loved it or hated it; those who preferred traditional locomotive lines were horrified.

The timing of the 'Silver Jubilee' required speeds of 70 to 75mph to be sustained up the 1-in-200 banks such as Stoke, with a 235 ton load behind the tender, while on the level, the schedule demanded sustained speeds of 85 to 90mph.

The A4s would be working their hardest at 75mph and above, in striking contrast to normal conditions on the heavy trains; and several key changes from the 66 A3s were made to the design. The exhaust was made freer by the use of 9in diameter piston valves, against the previous 8in, and the pressure drop between the boiler and the steam chest was virtually eliminated by streamlined passages, as well as by the increased fluidity of the steam itself, due to the higher boiler pressure of 250lb per sq in and a higher degree of superheat.

The softer blast resulting from the freer

exhaust would have created less draught in the firebox had the A3 boiler been retained, with, possibly, an adverse effect upon the steaming; so with the A4s, the boiler barrel was shortened from 19ft to 18ft, and the consequent reduction in tube heating surface was compensated for by the use of a combustion chamber. The cylinders of the A4s were slightly smaller, with an 18½in diameter against 19in.

The 'Silver Jubilee' made the A4s an overnight success.

A trial run on September 27, 1935, saw *Silver Link*, then just three weeks old, twice reach 112mph and sustain an average speed of 100mph for 43 consecutive miles on the ECML.

This run included an average of 108.7mph over the 10.6 miles from Biggleswade to St Neots, including several adverse gradients.

Three days later, No. 2509 made its debut on the 'Silver Jubilee' and undertook the 536½ mile daily return journey for the train's first two weeks without any mechanical troubles, which was indeed a great

ECML pioneer Gresley A3 Pacific No. 60096 *Papyrus* on the turntable at Dundee West sub shed on June 26, 1957. **BRIAN MORRISON**

A Newcastle to King's Cross express passes non-stop through Selby on May 22, 1959, powered by A4 class Pacific No. 60017 *Silver Fox*. This section of the ECML would later be diverted, avoiding the town. **BRIAN MORRISON**

tribute to design and workmanship.

The Jubilee year of George V saw Gresley bathe in a series of locomotive engineering triumphs, leading up to the aforementioned knighthood.

Four streamlined Pacifics were built for the Silver Jubilee service, three of which were stationed at King's Cross. The fourth, No. 2511 *Silver King*, was the spare engine and allocated to Gateshead shed, where it acted as pilot for the Up 'Jubilee', afterwards usually operating the Newcastle-Edinburgh-York-Newcastle turn beginning with the 11.10am non-stop express to Edinburgh.

In 1936, the LNER added a dynamometer car to the 'Silver Jubilee' increasing the load to 254 tons during trial runs between Newcastle and King's Cross and Newcastle and Edinburgh. The first run, on August 27, 1936, saw the newest A4 No. 2512 *Silver Fox* slightly improve on the maximum speed record of the previous September by hitting 113mph while going down Stoke Bank.

On the northbound trip on the same day, Silver Link made some outstanding running up the same incline. The 15.3 miles from Tallington to Stoke Summit were covered at an average speed of 82.7mph, with the locomotive working on 18% cut-off and a wide-open regulator. Both runs were made in ordinary service, but doubled up as trials to measure water and coal consumption, and to beat *Silver Link's* 112mph.

The LNER did not tell driver George Haygreen that a record attempt was to be attempted on Stoke Bank. Left in blissful oblivion, he neither had enough speed on the run up Stoke Bank, nor a sufficient reserve of boiler pressure.

Yet pushing hard, 113mph was reached, setting a British record for a steam train carrying fare-paying passengers.

The results of the trial were that the A4s were deemed to have a sufficient reserve of power, meaning that a 10-coach train would be totally practical for a proposed Glasgow-London service.

Between Newcastle and Edinburgh, No. 2511 *Silver King* made an exceptional climb of Cockburnspath Bank, keeping at 68mph up the 1-in-96 gradient.

In January 1937, a fifth A4 appeared in the form of No. 4482 *Golden Eagle*.

It was the first in a new series built both for the new 'Coronation' express and also on the fastest ordinary expresses.

However, the Great Western Railway had also upped the ante with its new 'Bristolian' service in September 1935. Ostensibly arranged to mark the 100th anniversary of the building of the GWR by Isambard Kingdom Brunel, it was also planned to start before the LNER's 'Silver Jubilee' at the end of the month.

The 'Bristolian' saw an express train scheduled to cover 118 miles in 105 minutes, with 69 miles to be run at nearly 80mph – and without a streamlined locomotive in sight. The trial train was made up of GWR 4-6-0 No. 6000 *King George V* hauling seven coaches, a total weight of 265 tons.

When the service began on September 9, the King maintained an overall average speed slightly higher than that of the 'Silver Jubilee'.

That is not to say that the GWR had dismissed streamlining. Experimental streamlined casings were applied in early 1935 to No. 6014 *King Henry VII* and No. 5005 *Manorbier Castle*; the bulbous domed addition to the smokebox door, fins extending behind the chimney and safety valve cover, coverings on the outside edge of the cylinders and a long straight splasher for each side.

However, the streamlining on both engines was abandoned in stages between then and 1943. A Down 'Bristolian' headed by non-streamlined No. 6027 *King Richard I* covered 90 miles at not less than 70mph, and faced with such performances, the GWR asked if air-smoothed casings would improve speed.

Streamlining was therefore left to the other three members of the 'Big Four'.

A4 No. 4499 *Pochard* at York in April 1938. The locomotive was renamed *Sir Murrough Wilson* a year later and was renumbered 60002 by British Railways. **COLOUR-RAIL**

The LNER named its A3 Pacifics after winning racehorses. No. 60093 *Coronach* won the Derby and St Leger in 1926. **THE RAILWAY MAGAZINE**

THE 'CORONATION' AND 'WEST RIDING LIMITED'

Named to mark the Coronation of King George VI, the 'Coronation' began running from King's Cross and Waverley from July 4, 1937. It left London at 4pm and arrived at 10pm.

The design of the train was based on the 'Silver Jubilee' but had a two-tone blue livery.

It comprised four sets of two-car articulated units, with a 'Beavertail' observation car with sloping back attached in the summer months.

Like the 'Silver Jubilee', it was decorated in art deco style. It was made up of Brake Third/Kitchen Third, Open First/Open First, Open Third/Kitchen Third and Open Third/Brake Third two-car articulated sets.

The train was for the most part hauled by A4s, the locomotive painted in a special garter blue livery with red wheels, a livery which later became standard for the class.

Encouraged by the success of the 'Silver Jubilee', the LNER provided even more lavish passenger accommodation on the 'Coronation', bringing the weight up to 312 tons against the previous 220 tons. The locomotives were asked to work harder and worked the six-hour trip King's Cross to London without being changed.

Facing cross winds, coal consumption could soar to the point where nearly all nine tons in the tender would be needed. On one occasion, the Up 'Coronation' ran out of coal at Hitchin.

The train ran until four days before the Second World War, during which the coaches were stored. Streamlined services ended on August 31, 1939, due to the enactment of the Emergency Powers (Defence) Act 1939. After this, passenger services were hurriedly pruned back, as evacuation trains had begun. In the months that followed, many services returned but by and large much slower than before the war, as freight was given precedence.

In 1948, several of the 'Coronation' vehicles returned to service used as general passenger stock, but never ran as a full set again. The two Beavertail observation cars

appeared on the West Highland lines in 1956, and are now preserved at Rothley on the Great Central Railway in Leicestershire.

Following on from the success of the 'Silver Jubilee' and the 'Coronation', the LNER introduced a streamlined service for Leeds and Bradford. Named the 'West Riding Limited', it began operating on September 27, 1937, with a train set in the same blue livery as the 'Coronation'.

Two new A4s were named after the woollen trade, from which the LNER aimed to attract business with the 'West Riding Limited'. No. 4495 *Great Snipe* was renamed *Golden Fleece*, while No. 4496 was named *Golden Shuttle* (later *Dwight D Eisenhower*).

OLD RIVALRIES REIGNITED

The exploits of *Flying Scotsman* and *Silver Link* also had the effect of beginning afresh the old competition between the operations of the ECML and WCML. The LMS watched record after record being broken, and acted to prevent them becoming a poor second in the London to Scotland stakes.

By 1936, LMS chief mechanical engineer William Stanier had already built a class of 13 new express passenger Pacific locomotives at Crewe Works to haul the 'Royal Scot' from Euston to Glasgow Central. They were known as the Princess Royal class because each of them was named after a princess.

As a response to the LNER streamlined expresses, the LMS planned a six-hour non-stop service from London to Glasgow, but needed to carry out tests to see if it was feasible.

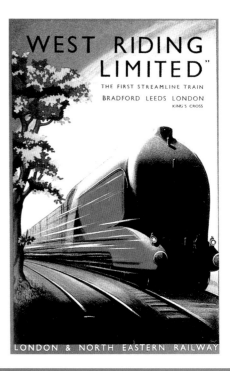

One of the two LNER Beavertail observation saloons at the Great Central Railway. **ROBIN JONES**

Tom Clark, the senior driver from Crewe North shed, was chosen to drive Princess Royal 4-6-2 No. 6201 *Princess Elizabeth* from Euston to Glasgow Central, with fireman Charles Fleet and passed fireman Albert Shaw making up the rest of his footplate crew.

On November 16, 1936, the trip was accomplished in a breathtaking five hours 53 minutes 38 seconds.

The following day, the return journey took five hours 44 minutes 14 seconds, achieving a Glasgow to London non-stop run with a 240 ton load at an average speed of 69mph. Clark's crew was instantly feted as national heroes, and national newspapers ran front page headlines proclaiming 'London-Glasgow Under 6 Hours', '401 Miles Non Stop', 'Railway Ambition Achieved'.

Stanier knew he had to up the ante still further if he was to compete with Gresley's A4s. He produced the first of the new streamlined Princess Coronation class Pacifics, No. 6220 *Coronation*. In 1937, Tom Clark was chosen to drive it and reclaim the world steam locomotive speed record.

The Coronations were an enlarged version of the Princess Royals and at 3300hp were the most powerful passenger steam locomotives ever built for the British main line. They matched the A4s in every respect.

The first five locomotives, Nos. 6220-4, were streamlined in a distinctive bulbous air-smoothed casing and painted Caledonian Railway blue with silver horizontal lines to match the 'Coronation Scot' train that they were intended to haul, although Stanier believed that the added weight and difficulty

in maintenance because of the streamlined casing was not offset by any benefits gained at high speed.

Tuesday, June 29, 1937, saw Tom Clark reach Euston from Crewe, a distance of 158 miles, in two hours 9 minutes 45 seconds, with the press trip preceding the launch of the 'Coronation Scot' on July 5. He made it back to Crewe in one hour 59 minutes and reclaimed the record with a top speed of 114mph, just south of the town. History relates that Clark did not allow sufficient braking distance before entering a series of crossover points on the approach to Crewe, or even attempt to observe the speed limit as the train approached the station, and the crockery in the dining car came crashing down before Clark slowed to 52mph.

The return trip from Crewe back to London was covered in 119 minutes, an

average of 79.7mph, making it one of the fastest ever recorded in Britain. The highlight was the 69.9 miles from Walton to Willesden Junction, which took 47 minutes and 1 second at an average of 89.3mph, with a maximum speed of 100mph at Castlethorpe water troughs. Accordingly, the LMS could claim the fastest start-to-stop runs of over 100 and 150 miles. Two days later, a press trip for the LNER's 'Coronation' hauled by No. 4489 *Dominion of Canada* tried to reclaim the record, but could manage only 109.5mph on Stoke Bank.

The crockery incident led to the LMS and LNER reaching an agreement to end further potentially dangerous record-breaking runs for the sake of publicity.

That did not stop the LNER regaining the world speed record little over a year later, and holding it for all time.

MALLARD:
THE CROWNING GLORY

Germany's production of the Flying Hamburger diesel railcar set had led the country to see if similar speeds could be achieved with streamlined steam locomotives. The Borsig locomotive works accordingly turned out three streamliners which became Class 05.

The second of these, No. 05002, seized the world steam locomotive speed record on May 11, 1936, when it reached 124.5mph while hauling a 197 ton train on the Berlin–Hamburg line.

On May 30, 1936, No. 05002 established an unbroken start stop speed record for steam locomotives when, during the return leg of a Berlin-Hamburg test run, it covered the 70.1 miles from Wittenberge to a signal stop before Berlin-Spandau in 48 minutes 32 seconds at an average start-stop speed of 86.66mph.

The downside of increasing locomotive speeds was that braking distances were getting longer and so braking systems had to be improved.

Gresley looked at the Westinghouse system used by his rival the LMS and arranged a series of trials, which involved rapid acceleration followed by the brake test.

On July 3, 1938, the Westinghouse team arrived at Wood Green sidings in London to find A4 No. 4468 *Mallard*, which had been outshopped only four months earlier and was the first of the class to be fitted with the Kylchap double-blast pipe, hence its selection for the record run.

It was coupled to teak dynamometer car No. 902502, behind which were three twin sets of carriages from the 'Coronation' set.

Gresley missed the big day, because he was ill at home.

Again, the true purpose of the trip was not revealed to the footplate crew – led by

This sign has been erected at the spot on Stoke Bank near Carlby south of Little Bytham near milepost 90¼, where *Mallard* reached 126mph. **NETWORK RAIL**

Doncaster driver Joe Duddington, who had a reputation for running trains hard when needed, and including fireman Tommy Bray and inspector Sam Jenkins – or the Westinghouse team until the train had left Wood Green at 11.46am.

Why not? It may be the LNER did not want the LMS to hear about the planned attempt beforehand, or because the LNER's civil engineering department may complain, as the track had an official speed limit of only 90mph!

The outward journey involved a series of ordinary brake tests. The run ended at Barkston, where the locomotive and dynamometer car were turned on the triangle. The Westinghouse team members were offered a taxi to Peterborough if they

did not want to ride on the train as it attempted to retake the speed record on the way back, but every one of them refused.

The train departed from Barkston South Junction at 4.15pm, when tea was served in the first class section.

The crew was dismayed to find speed limits in force at Grantham due to permanent way work and the station was passed at just 18mph. But fireman Bray used the time to build a big fire. By Duddington, *Mallard* had reached 65mph, with its boiler at full pressure. The engine accelerated up to Stoke summit and passed Stoke signalbox at 85mph.

The train then entered Stoke Tunnel, and before the guard switched on the lights, passengers were delighted by a firework display of red-hot cinders passing the windows after flying from *Mallard's* twin chimneys.

The record keepers inside the dynamometer car saw that the A4 had passed Stoke summit at 6mph faster than *Silver Fox* when it set its record.

Mallard then accelerated down Stoke Bank, faster than *Silver Fox* had done.

Within minutes, the speedometer reached 120mph, beating the LMS record. But Duddington and Bray knew that they had to do more.

For one quarter of a mile, the needle in the dynamometer car recorded 126mph, at milepost 90¼, between Little Bytham and Essendine. The German record had now been broken as well.

Gresley's assistant Douglas Edge was asked if the crew should try to go one better and hit 130mph, but with Essendine Tunnel approaching, he made the painful safety first decision and the message was conveyed to Duddington to shut off.

Essendine, the only station on the ECML serving the tiny county of Rutland, was still passed at 108mph.

Minutes later, a distinctive smell conveyed the bad news of the day. The A4's big end had run hot and it had to slow down as much as possible to reach Peterborough

The village of Offord Cluny, midway between Huntingdon and St Neots, may have lost its local station, Offord & Buckden, on the ECML on February 2, 1959, when it was among several little-used stops that were closed in order to help speed up times, but it is undoubtedly proud nonetheless of its LNER heritage, as this *Mallard*-themed village sign shows. **ROBIN JONES**

A4 No. 60022 *Mallard* departs from Edinburgh Waverley in September 1961. **COLOUR-RAIL**

to avoid being wrecked. There, it was found that the white metal had melted and an ageing Ivatt Atlantic, No. 3290, was called upon to take the train back to King's Cross.

Edge telephoned Gresley to convey the news. Meanwhile, the records from the dynamometer were read and it was found that 126mph had been reached, but for just one second over 60 yards. The LNER claimed only a peak average of 125mph.

In those days there was no internet or satellite TV, but within hours of the train arriving back in London, *Mallard's* feat was making headline news around the world. The press named *Mallard* the 'Blue Streak', a nickname which has stuck for the A4s. The silence from the German media and Nazi propaganda top brass was deafening.

Britain had invented the steam railway engine through Richard Trevithick in 1802, at Coalbrookdale in Shropshire, and 136 years later, the country's finest steam locomotive was proudly sitting on the top of the world.

The overheated bearing was quickly remetalled and *Mallard* returned to service within nine days.

Gresley planned to try to set another new record in September 1939, but these plans were thwarted by the outbreak of the Second World War. Before *Mallard's* record run, it was calculated that 130mph was possible with an A4.

Looking northwards up Stoke Bank, the world's greatest steam railway racetrack, from a bridge next to the Lincolnshire village of Swayfield in September 2011. Running south is the Network Rail New Measurement Train which assesses the condition of track so that engineers can determine where to work, and is a specially converted High Speed Train comprising two Class 43 power cars and Mk3 coaches. The train measures the contact between rails, wheels and the overhead electric supply line, along with track geometry and overhead line height and stagger. **ROBIN JONES**

COCK O'THE NORTH

Double-headed Pacifics had been barred from the ECML 'extension' to Aberdeen because of their combined axle loading, so Gresley came up with a new kind of locomotive that had never been seen in Britain before.

The steep gradients and tight curves on the Edinburgh to Aberdeen main line were tackled by double heading two smaller engines on express passenger trains. Gresley recognised this was a waste of resources and came up with one engine that could do the job – the P2 2-8-2 or Mikado.

The LNER became the only company in Britain to run Mikados, an American design. The first 2-8-2 locomotive was built in 1884 and the name Mikado originates from a group of Baldwin locomotives supplied in 1897 to the 3ft 6in gauge Nippon Railway of

Japan. The Gilbert and Sullivan opera *The Mikado* had been a huge hit in the US, and the name stuck to these exports.

Gresley's Mikado design, drawn up in 1932, had four driving axles for greater adhesion but used an A3-type boiler and double chimney.

The first to appear was No. 2001 *Cock o' the North* in May 1934. After early problems were ironed out, following a visit to the locomotive testing station at Vitry-sur-Seine near Paris for two months of trials, it entered service in Scotland. A second and slightly modified P2, No. 2002 *Earl Marischal*, and another four followed in 1936, each with small differences between them, and resembling the A4 Pacifics.

Like the A4s, the P2s were a significant forward for British locomotive design, and spent their entire working lives on the Aberdeen route.

STOKE BANK'S LAST STEAM RECORD

A total of 35 A4 Pacifics were built, although one of them, No. 4469 *Sir Ralph Wedgwood*, originally named *Gadwall*, was scrapped after bomb damage in June 1942, with the name switched to No. 4466 *Herring Gull*.

Among them was No. 4498, the 100th Gresley Pacific built, which honoured its designer in being named after him. It was originally due to be named *Bittern*, in line with the bird theme, until an LNER enthusiast member of the Railway Correspondence and Travel Society suggested that it should be named *Sir Nigel Gresley*. The name *Bittern* was later given to No. 4464, later No. 60019.

Mallard's record was never broken; indeed, the will to set new steam records vanished in the aftermath of the Second World War. Sir Nigel Gresley the man died after a short illness on April 5, 1941, and was buried in Netherseal.

King's Cross-based A4 4-6-2 No. 60032 *Gannet* bursts out of Stoke Tunnel at the head of a 13-coach express bound for London on July 21, 1962. **GAVIN MORRISON**

The second Gresley P2 express engine for the Aberdeen route, No. 2002 *Earl Marischal*.
OS NOCK/THE RAILWAY MAGAZINE

Having climbed Stoke Bank, King's Cross-based A3 Pacific No. 60061 *Pretty Polly* approaches Stoke Tunnel on July 21, 1962. **GAVIN MORRISON**

No. 4498 *Sir Nigel Gresley* was allocated to King's Cross shed from new, and had a spell at Grantham between April 1944 and June 1950.

In November 1955, it was said that driver Bill Hoole took No. 60007 down Stoke Bank at a speed of 117mph with the 'Tees-Tyne Pullman', well above the 90mph limit. A civil engineer with a Hallade track recording instrument was on board the train; however, the device was not designed for recording such speeds and disciplinary action against the footplate crew was avoided because its accuracy was questioned.

As express diesels arrived on the ECML in the autumn of 1958, a farewell high-speed steam trip to coincide with the Golden Jubilee of the Stephenson Locomotive Society was arranged. *Sir Nigel Gresley* and Bill Hoole were chosen, and No. 60007 was given an overhaul at Doncaster Works.

The civil engineer gave his consent for the speed limits to be relaxed over certain sections and a maximum of 110mph was permitted down Stoke Bank.

The eight-coach train departed King's Cross on Saturday, May 23, 1959, with Hoole on the regulator, assisted by fireman Alf Hancox.

It was claimed that it reached 100mph after Stevenage on the outward journey to Doncaster. The train made a spectacular climb on Stoke Bank, reaching 83mph between Essendine and Little Bytham.

On the way back, Stoke summit was passed at 75mph, rising to 99mph before Corby Glen, and 109mph by Little Bytham.

Bill Hoole appeared as if he was going for the record, but those in control were concerned about the safety of the 400 passengers on board and would not allow him to go beyond the officially sanctioned limit of the day.

When the train reached 112mph, Alan Pegler, a member of the Eastern Region board, who was also on the footplate, signalled to Inspector Bert Dixon that the driver must ease off at this point.

The 12.3 miles from Corby Glen to Tallington were covered in just seven minutes six seconds at an average of 104mph, possibly the fastest ever time between those points by a steam locomotive, beating even *Mallard* in this respect.

Southwards, beyond Tempsford, 100mph was reached for the third time in the trip. The train arrived back at King's Cross four minutes early, having taken in 137 minutes 38 seconds from Doncaster, an average of 68mph over the 156 miles.

In the case of *Sir Nigel Gresley*, there was no hot big end. And so a new official post-war steam record of 112mph was set.

Lined up outside King's Cross shed (34A) on May 9, 1954, are A1 Pacific No. 60155 *Borderer*, V2 2-6-2 No. 60903 and A4 Pacific No. 60034 *Lord Faringdon*. **BRIAN MORRISON**

THE LAST EAST COAST PACIFICS

Following the death of Gresley, Edward Thompson became chief mechanical engineer and began his standardisation plans.

The standardisation policy began with a new mixed traffic Pacific, the A2/2.

There was no room for Gresley's P2 2-8-2-s; despite their innovative design, Thompson had them all rebuilt as Pacifics between 1943-45, as A2/2s. They were non-streamlined with Walschaerts valve gear on the centre cylinder. Although they returned to work the Edinburgh-Aberdeen line, in late 1949 they were transferred to England and divided between York and New England (Peterborough) sheds. The engines were withdrawn between 1959-61.

The A2/2 class also included Thompson's version of Gresley's V2 2-6-2, the last four of which on the order books Thompson ordered to be built at Darlington to an A2/1 design, between 1944/45.

The four A2/1s worked express passenger and express goods trains. All of them were withdrawn between August 1960 and February 1961.

In 1944, Thompson went ahead with the building of 15 standard Pacifics based on his A2/2 design. These, the A2/3s, were the first new Pacifics built at Doncaster for eight years and included several innovations, including steam brakes, a hopper ashpan, electric lighting, and a self-cleaning smokebox. The first A2/3s were withdrawn from service in

1962, and the last were withdrawn in 1965.

After Thompson retired and was replaced by Arthur H Peppercorn, the last LNER CME, a second batch of 15 Thompson A2/3s and a further 13 ordered in 1945 were built to a modified design. The first Peppercorn A2, as they were known, appeared in 1948.

The A2s allocated to England worked services, including express passenger, slow passenger, and parcel services.

Allocated to York, No. 60526 *Sugar Palm* was often used to replace locomotives that failed on the ECML.

In 1961, it set a speed record for the class of 101mph while descending Stoke Bank.

The last three remaining A2s were withdrawn from Scotland in 1966. One of them, No. 60532 *Blue Peter*, has been preserved, but at the time of writing has been awaiting a £500,000 overhaul for many years.

The long-running BBC TV children's programme *Blue Peter* helped raise money towards its first heritage era overhaul in the early Seventies.

Peppercorn's biggest class was his A1 express passenger Pacifics, not to be confused with Gresley's original A1s, most of which had by the time of Peppercorn's appointment been rebuilt as A3s. The few that had not had been redesignated by Thompson as A10s in preparation for the new A1.

The Peppercorn A1 had its roots in the rebuilding by Thompson of the first Gresley Pacific, *Great Northern*, in 1945. The rebuild was meant to be the start of a new A1 class, but it was not repeated, and the sole class member was designated A1/1. Instead, 49 locomotives were built to a new design by Peppercorn.

They were designed to cope with the heaviest passenger trains on the ECML and

The last of the great ECML Pacifics were the Peppercorn A1s. No. 60116 is seen passing a snowbound Retford on New Year's Eve 1948 with the Up 'Tees-Tyne Pullman.' **THE RAILWAY MAGAZINE**

on to Aberdeen, often up to 15 coaches long and weighing up to 550 tons. They were able to haul trains of this size on the level at speeds of up to 70mph, and very economically too.

Nearly-new No. 60114 was tested between King's Cross, Grantham and Leeds in 1949, and consumed an average of 40.2lb per mile of coal on 490 ton trains and 47.5lb per mile on trains of more, comparing very favourably with the A4s.

Like the LNER Pacifics that had gone before, they had a three-cylinder arrangement and they were fitted with double Kylchap chimneys.

Ordered by the LNER, the Peppercorn A1s were delivered from Doncaster and Darlington Works after nationalisation on January 1, 1948.

They were renowned above everything else for their reliability, averaging over 200 miles a day, a far better statistic than accrued by any other steam engine on British Railways. No. 60156 *Great Central* of King's Cross shed ran 96,000 miles on one year alone.

They could handle any job that was given them, no matter how hard, but despite their success, they came up against the biggest stumbling block of all – dieselisation. By 1966, all of them had been scrapped.

Above: One of the most successful classes designed by Gresley were the V2 2-6-2s, the first and sole surviving member of which, No. 60800 (4771) *Green Arrow*, which is now part of the National Collection, is seen at King's Cross. The V2s were the LNER's most famous mixed traffic design, which dated back to 1932 and included the classic Gresley wide firebox. At one stage it was planned to streamline them like the A4s, but in the end only the partially streamlined A4 cab was kept, along with the partly hidden steam pipe covers to the cylinders. A total of 184 V2s in 11 batches were built between 1936 and 1944. Most were allocated to sheds along the ECML and between Edinburgh and Aberdeen. *Green Arrow* acquired fame by hauling the first leg of the King's Cross to Glasgow express goods. However, they could also do passenger work and occasionally replaced not only the A1/A3 Pacifics but also the streamlined A4s. During the Second World War, the V2s hauled many heavy passenger trains. The last V2 to be withdrawn was No. 60831 on December 6, 1966; it was also the last of Gresley's big engines to be withdrawn. **BRIAN SHARPE**

Above left: The sole A1/1 Pacific No. 60113 *Great Northern* makes the scheduled stop at York on August 29, 1954, heading an express from King's Cross to Newcastle. The locomotive was a Thompson rebuild of a Gresley A10 Pacific that was then developed by Peppercorn as the eventual new A1 class. **BRIAN MORRISON**

German Class 05 steam engine No. 05001 at the Deutsche Bundesbahn Museum in Nuremberg. It is the surviving sister locomotive of No. 05002, which lost the world record to Mallard and was scrapped in 1960. **DOCO/CREATIVE COMMONS**

New York Central & Hudson River Railroad No. 999 in Syracuse three days after making its record run on May 13, 1893.

WAS *MALLARD* THE FASTEST?

It goes without saying that there can be a huge gulf in credibility between official speed records and unofficial ones. Concrete evidence can be produced to back up the former, while the latter can rely on anything from amateur but well-meaning measurements to mere lineside gossip and speculation.

There were times when the trend among railways was not to boast about speed records, for fear of deterring the public from travelling. How many test run speed achievements were unrecorded and unreported in such circumstances we can only guess.

There are many anecdotal stories of locomotive crews reaching high speeds with the incident quickly played down for fear of disciplinary action.

One of the earliest unofficial record breakers was New York Central & Hudson River Railroad 4-4-0 No. 999 which was claimed to have reached 112mph during an exhibition run of the 'Empire State Express' between Batavia and Buffalo on May 10, 1893, the year in which the locomotive was built. If the unofficial timers were right, No. 999 would have become the world's first object on wheels to exceed 100mph.

Earlier, on September 14, 1891, the 'Empire State Express' was said to have run the 436 miles from New York City to Buffalo in seven hours six minutes, with an officially recorded top speed of 82mph, thereby setting a new world record in itself. The feat was the product of competition with the Pennsylvania Railroad in the build-up to the Chicago World's Fair in 1893 which marked the 400th anniversary of Christopher Columbus's arrival in the New World in 1492.

No. 999 was preserved in 1962, and is now displayed inside the main hall at the Chicago Museum of Science and Industry.

The special train on July 23, 1959, pictured just before reaching 112mph on Stoke Bank. **PH WELLS**

Driver Arthur Taylor joined the GNR as an engine cleaner at King's Cross on February 2, 1895, and worked his way up to becoming a regular driver on July 24, 1912. Driving A1 Pacific No. 4476 *Royal Lancer*, he handled East Coast expresses like the 'Flying Scotsman', 'Silver Jubilee' and 'Coronation'. He was in charge of No. 2509 *Silver Link* on September 27, 1935, when it twice reached 112½mph and attained an average speed of 107½mph over a 25-mile section of the ECML. He received an OBE in 1935 and retired six years later.
THE RAILWAY MAGAZINE

The locomotive that represents alleged record-breaker No. 7002 in the Railroad Museum of Pennsylvania.

It was also claimed that Pennsylvania Railroad E2 class 4-4-2 No. 7002 reached 127.1mph at Crestline in Ohio while hauling its 18 hour 'Pennsylvania Special' from New York City to Chicago on June 11, 1905. However, engines did not carry speedometers at the time, and speed was calculated by measuring time between mile markers, so the 'record' was never official. The New York Times said on June 14, 1905, that the claims published in the Chicago press had been exaggerated with the speed nearer 70-80mph.

No. 7002 was built in 1902, but despite its claim to fame, was scrapped in 1935. However, 1902-built E2a class 4-4-2 No. 8063, later rebuilt to an E7, was cosmetically altered to resemble No. 7002 and displayed both at the 1939 New York World's Fair and the Chicago Railroad Fair in 1948/49. It is now in the Railroad Museum of Pennsylvania.

On July 20, 1934, Chicago, Milwaukee, St Paul and Pacific Railroad 4-6-4 No. 6402 was tested in order to show that a high-speed service was feasible. Heading a regular service train from Chicago, to Milwaukee, it hauled the 380-ton train over the 85 minutes in 67 minutes and 37 seconds. A maximum speed of 103mph was reached.

It also averaged 89.92mph for a 68.9 mile length. British author Bryan Benn

believes it is the first claim of more than 100mph (in which the surviving documentation strongly indicates its accuracy), and therefore it may be deemed by some to have beaten *Flying Scotsman* by a few months. The success of the test run led to the railroad launching its 'Hiawatha' express in 1935.

The railroad had four streamlined Alco 4-4-2s built to haul this express. They were the world's first locomotives built for daily operation at more than 100mph, with a 6½ hour run between Minneapolis and Chicago, and designed for 120mph.

At the time, the 'Hiawatha' was the fastest scheduled express train in the world.

A recorded run with a dynamometer car behind locomotive No. 2 on May 15, 1935, from Milwaukee and Wisconsin saw 112.5mph recorded over a 14 mile stretch. As such, it would have been the first steam locomotive to officially exceed 110mph.

They were followed in service by the six F7 streamlined 4-6-4s which were introduced in 1939 and ran at speeds in excess of 100mph

on a daily basis. One was recorded at 125mph on a run between Chicago and Milwaukee after managing an average of 120mph for 4½ miles, a whisker short of *Mallard's* record. The F7s were also recorded as running to the fastest scheduled speed between stations; the 'Twin Cities Hiawatha' had to cover the 78 miles from Portage to Sparta in 58 minutes at an average of 81mph.

An F7 class streamlined 'Hiawatha' locomotive pictured in 1937 as it was being moved out of the Alco factory. **OTTO KUHLER/CREATIVE COMMONS**

Streamlined A4 Pacific No. 2509
Silver Link at Grantham in 1937.
COLOUR-RAIL

TOP SHED: HOME OF THE RECORD BREAKERS

Central to many of the express trains and steam record breakers on the ECML was one of the most famous engine sheds of all – King's Cross.

Known as 'Top Shed', it was built as 'engine stables' in 1850 when the GNR opened its main line, right up to 1963 when a new diesel depot was established at Finsbury Park to the north.

Top Shed lay three quarters of a mile to the north of the existing King's Cross station, near the original Maiden Lane terminus.

As built, the shed had 25 roads, plus an 11-road repair shop in the centre. A large part of the original building remained in use until 1963. The King's Cross goods yard lay next door.

In 1851, a turntable was installed; prior to that, tender first running had been accepted practice.

Six years later, the Midland Railway reached agreement with the GNR to run over its main line from King's Cross to Hitching, and accordingly, had its own roundhouse built at Top Shed. The Midland stopped using the GNR main line from October 1, 1868, when its own route into St Pancras opened, and so the GNR inherited the roundhouse, which remained in use until 1931, when it was dismantled.

Top Shed handed numerous types of locomotives, not only for the ECML but also for London suburban working too. However, its biggest claim to fame lay with the great Pacifics. In 1927, the longest non-stop engine

duty in Britain was the 9.450am relief 'Flying Scotsman' from King's Cross to Newcastle. Top Shed crews lodged overnight at Newcastle and returned the next day, setting the pattern for future non-stop working such as the 'Flying Scotsman' over the whole length of the ECML to Edinburgh in summer 1928.

Gresley frequently met the Top Shed drivers and encouraged them in their work. It was a King's Cross crew, of driver A Taylor and fireman J Luty, who took No. 2509 *Silver Link* and the 'Silver Jubilee to the new record of 112½mph on September 27, 1935.

In the heyday of steam in the Thirties, Top Shed had a superb record of turning out locomotives for prolonged duties. In 1937, King's Cross-based A4 No. 4492 *Dominion of New Zealand* worked to Edinburgh on 44 days in a row non-stop. Indeed, an A4 could return from one trip and be ready to embark on another from Top Shed within a few hours

Out of the class of 35 A4s, before the Second World War, King's Cross had 11 of them allocated to it.

In 1948, when flooding swept away part of the ECML north of Berwick, the longest non-stop run worked by Top Shed crews was extended to 408½ miles, because of the diversion of Edinburgh-bound trains from Newcastle through Carlisle and Carstairs.

The demise of Top Shed began in 1958 with the arrival of four English Electric Type 4 diesel electrics to work passenger trains, while the following spring, other diesels arrived to handle suburban traffic.

The shed was closed on June 16, 1963, when scheduled steam services in and out of King's Cross ended.

The buildings which had comprised one of the proudest locomotive sheds in the world were demolished soon afterwards. ∎

A4 4-6-2 No. 4902 *Seagull* leaves Grantham with the 1.20pm down 'Flying Scotsman'.
OS NOCK/THE RAILWAY MAGAZINE

King's Cross shed was reached by a branch off the main line at Belle Isle, between Gasworks and Copenhagen Tunnels. Here Peterborough's A2 Pacific No. 60513 *Dante* is coaled up for a return journey north on May 9, 1954. **BRIAN MORRISON**

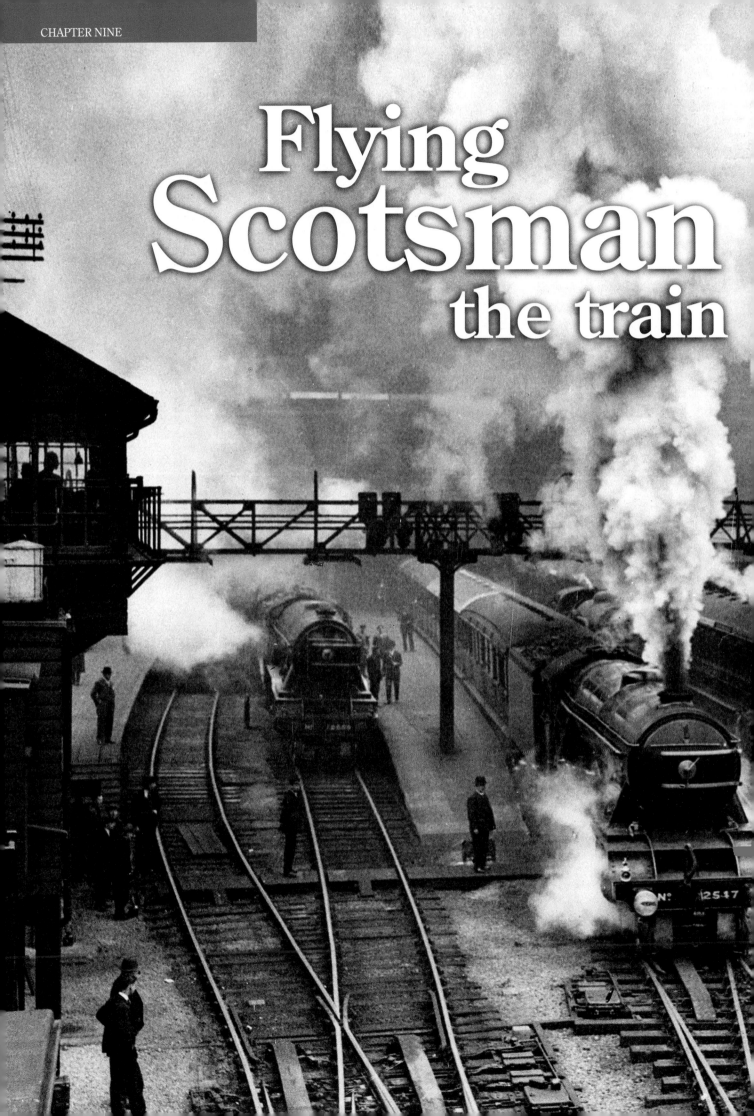

CHAPTER NINE

Flying Scotsman
the train

A hand-coloured postcard of Ivatt C2 4-4-0 No. 990 hauling the 'Flying Scotsman' through Hatfield. **ROBIN JONES COLLECTION**

The East Coast Main Line is often referred to as the route of the 'Flying Scotsman'. While it is certainly true that LNER A1, later A3, Pacific No. 4472 *Flying Scotsman* plied its trade on the line, the slogan refers to one of the world's most famous named trains, which preceded the building of the locomotive in 1923 by more than half a century.

The named train has its beginnings in the aforementioned decision by the Great Northern, North Eastern and North British railways to establish the East Coast Joint Stock fleet of carriages in 1860, to help facilitate through running and eliminate changes of trains.

The moved paved the way for the GNR to run its first 'Special Scotch Express' in 1862, with simultaneous departures at 10am from King's Cross and Edinburgh Waverley.

At first, the whole journey took 10½ hours, including a 30 minute stop at York for lunch. However, improvements in all aspects of railway technology, including in 1870 the addition of the Stirling singles, saw this speeded up to 8½ hours by the time that the first Race to the North took place in 1888.

From about 1870, the train became colloquially known as the 'Flying Scotsman'.

The train received a major facelift in 1900. Dining cars were added, carriages were heated and corridor connections meant that it was possible to walk between vehicles.

The availability of lunch on board halved the stop at York, although the total journey time remained at 8½ hours. Introduced in 1897 were the first British Atlantic locomotives, the Ivatt C2 4-4-0s.

At the Grouping of 1923, the GNR, NER and North British all became part of one of the 'Big Four' – the London & North Eastern Railway, which also inherited the East Coast Joint Stock.

LNER A1 Pacific No. 4475 *Flying Fox* (right) departs King's Cross with the 'Flying Scotsman' in 1930. To the left is sister locomotive No. 2547 *Doncaster*, also named after a racehorse as per LNER policy for this class. **NRM**

A SMART TURN OUT

"THE FLYING SCOTSMAN"

LEAVES KING'S CROSS LONDON
AND WAVERLEY STATION EDINBURGH
EVERY WEEKDAY AT 10 A.M.

LONDON & NORTH EASTERN RAILWAY

The 'Flying Scotsman', LNER poster, c1935. **NRM**

The LNER gave the train a major revamp in 1924, officially renaming it the 'Flying Scotsman' for the first time.

To add further prestige, it was decided to name one of LNER chief mechanical engineer Sir Nigel Gresley's new A1 Pacifics which had been designed at the latter end of the GNR days after the train.

The locomotive, No. 1472, was displayed at the British Empire Exhibition at Wembley in 1924.

Because of the post-Races to the North agreement not to cut the eight hours 15 minutes time for the London to Edinburgh journey, up to this point the speed of the train had been restricted.

However, after valve gear modifications, the coal consumption of the A1 class was greatly reduced to the point where the service could be run nonstop with just one fully-laden coal tender. Also, 10 tenders were specially built for the launch of the 'Flying Scotsman' with a coal capacity of nine tons instead of the usual eight.

Ten locomotives of classes A1 and A3 were provided with corridor tenders for use on the service. These allowed relief footplate crews to ride on the train and take over halfway, cutting fatigue levels.

The locomotive *Flying Scotsman*, by then renumbered 4472, hauled the first of its namesake trains from London on May 1, 1928.

History was made: it was the first nonstop run of a scheduled service over the whole length of 393 miles. However, West Coast rival the London Midland & Scottish Railway had four days earlier run the Edinburgh section of its 'Royal Scot' all 399.7 miles from Euston.

The new nonstop service also boasted improved catering, and among its many onboard services was a barber's shop.

This splendidly restored LNER Gresley teak buffet car is one of many jewels in the crown of the Bo'ness & Kinneil Railway near Edinburgh and its Scottish Railway Exhibition. The vehicle was built at York in 1937 and preserved in 1977. It contains a kitchen, a serving counter and passenger seating, and was used on long-distance and express services all over the LNER system, including the East Coast main line. These buffet cars were the longest-lasting Gresley coaches in traffic, and some lasted long enough to be painted in the BR blue and grey corporate colours. They were the last wooden-bodied coaches on British Rail when they were withdrawn in 1977, although No. 644 has run as a buffet car on Scottish Railway Preservation Society main line railtours. **ROBIN JONES**

THE RAILWAY CATERING SYSTEM

Just as the coaching inns on the Great North Road had provided refreshments and meals, so the railways that replaced the stagecoach routes had to provide catering, and ensure that standards and facilities were forever improving as the network evolved.

The big advantage of course was that trains could serve meals on board, without passengers have to disembark at a hostelry where they would probably spend the night too, lengthening the journey.

Britain's early inter-city railways often provided 15- or 20-minute stops for sustenance at particular stations. However, the big drawback was late arrivals would mean there would not be enough time for passengers to be served, and there were complaints that the soup was served so hot, and people had to wait so long before it was

AN LNER chef waits at the door of his Edinburgh-bound kitchen car in the Twenties. **THE RAILWAY MAGAZINE**

Rolls entering the oven in an LNER bakery. **THE RAILWAY MAGAZINE**

The Frigidaire plant in an LNER kitchen car. **THE RAILWAY MAGAZINE**

Driving Van Trailer No. 82205, part of the new East Coast 'Flying Scotsman' set, at King's Cross on September 18, 2011. **ROBIN JONES**

The 'Flying Scotsman' first-class car with movable armchair seats pictured in 1928. **THE RAILWAY MAGAZINE**

The interior of a 1928 'Flying Scotsman' third-class coach. **THE RAILWAY MAGAZINE**

cool, that the departure bell rang long before they had had a chance to attack the rest of the meal. Nonetheless, such refreshment stops – York was the main one on the ECML – lasted until the early 20th century.

The solution was to serve meals on board.

It was the Great Northern Railway that introduced the first restaurant car, for first-class passengers only. It was introduced on King's Cross to Leeds services in 1879.

The catering operation of the restaurant car was leased to a contractor, which supplied the food and cooked the meals in a little coke range. This first vehicle could seat only 19 diners.

A big disadvantage was that corridor coaches had not been introduced at the time, and passengers who wanted to eat on board had to travel in the restaurant car throughout the journey.

The introduction of corridor connections saw the concept finally take off big time, with most British express trains including restaurant cars.

By the 1920s, gas or electric cookers had taken the place of the old coke fire or coal range, and the menus were as varied as those in any first-class hotel.

Just as the coaching inns had their system of arranging refreshments, so the railway companies built up their own extensive catering networks.

Behind the scenes at the big terminal stations, and certain important intermediate places, were a chain of depots, where the chefs and conductors of the restaurant cars were supplied with their provisions. The system was focused on the kitchens where the head chef planned out the menus, often three days ahead.

Soups, sauces and sweets, such as tarts and puddings, were made in the central kitchens in order to relieve the chefs on the trains of as much work as possible, but joints, poultry, fish, vegetables and other sundries of the meals which require cooking were cooked while the train was running. However, where a train started from one of the depot stations just at dinner time, the joints were sent on board ready cooked, and needed only to be kept hot.

Sometimes the head chef had to prepare special menus for royalty or VIP travellers, often with particular tastes.

As soon as the menus were announced by the head chef, purchasers got to work, and supplies from butchers, greengrocers, fishmongers and all the other gastronomic merchants flowed into the depots. Every effort was made to ensure that supplies were delivered at the last available moment before they are required on the trains, so that the food may be served up fresh.

By the Twenties, restaurant cars were far bigger than the first in 1879. The LNER ran the latest all-electric restaurant cars on the ECML, and staff could serve breakfast, lunch or dinner to 78 travellers at one sitting. A separate kitchen car was placed between the first class and third class restaurant carriages, forming a set of three articulated vehicles carried on four bogies, improving the steadiness of the cars for the benefit of staff and diners alike.

Electricity was generated for cooking and lighting by dynamos beneath the floor, connected to belts from the axles of the cars. Hotplates, heated cupboards for warming plates, urns, kettles, were all worked by electricity.

Two 45 gallon tanks for warm water storage were fitted in the roof of the corridor just outside the kitchen. Electrical elements fastened to the underside of these tanks were connected to a boiler on top of the main oven, ensuring continuous boiling water for washing dishes. A later Twenties innovation was a plant for making ice cream. It was worked by an electrically driven compressor.

Railway laundries based at various points on the system were responsible for the pure white table cloths and table napkins in the restaurant cars, as well as the vast amount of linen used in the refreshment rooms, hotels and steamers.

The most important stations, and especially those at junctions, were provided with refreshment rooms, just like the stagecoach inns of old. The LNER boasted that most of the customers were not railway travellers but local businessmen and residents who preferred the standard of the food to that served by other establishments in their town.

The railways also had huge bakeries to produce buns, rolls, pies and pastries – both for serving on board and in these restaurant rooms. During the night, railway bakers worked to produce them from the basic ingredients for serving fresh the following day. Brown rolls or buns were raked from the ovens into waiting baskets to be taken away by van and barrow to the first trains.

Supplies were sent out at stated intervals during the day to the restaurant cars, refreshment rooms and hotels.

The coaching inns of the Great North Road had not exactly gone away: the services that they provided had simply evolved into operations of industrial scale as the railways carried infinitely more passengers at faster speeds, and in terms of standards of luxury, the 'Flying Scotsman' raised the game, big time.

THE

FLYING SCOTSMAN

1862 - 1962

British Railways poster celebrating the centenary of the 'Flying Scotsman' in 1962. The locomotives shown are a GNR Stirling Single and a Deltic. **NRM**

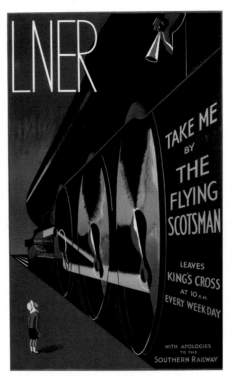

Take me by the 'Flying Scotsman', LNER poster, 1932. **NRM**

SPEEDING UP AGAIN

As we will see, the old Races to the North rivalry flared up again shortly afterwards. The speed restriction agreement was ended in 1932, and in that year, the scheduled time for the 'Flying Scotsman' was reduced to seven hours 30 minutes, and six years later, to seven hours 20 minutes.

Following nationalisation, the 'Flying Scotsman' ceased to be a nonstop named train, and called at Peterborough, York and Newcastle en route.

When dieselisation saw the new Deltics replace steam, the train became a focal point of an advertising campaign, just as it had been in 1928.

After British Rail was privatised, former ECML operator the Great North Eastern Railway continued using the name from 1996 to November 2007, and even branded itself The Route of the Flying Scotsman. Its successor on the route, National Express East Coast, continued using the name until November 2009, when the franchise was taken back by the government and handed to a new publicly owned operator, East Coast.

The 'Flying Scotsman' was relaunched by East Coast on May 23, 2011.

Using Class 91 electric locomotives, the new service could leave Edinburgh at 5.40am and be at King's Cross exactly four hours later, despite stopping at Newcastle.

Furthermore, a new 6am service from Berwick-upon-Tweed connects to the 'Flying Scotsman' and provides passengers from Northumberland stations with a rail journey into London before 10am for the first time in decades. East Coast boasted that the train

> **IN TERMS OF STANDARDS OF LUXURY, THE 'FLYING SCOTSMAN' RAISED THE GAME, BIG TIME.**

Without a trace of exhaust on a hot summer's day, A4 No. 60013 *Dominion of New Zealand* approaches Doncaster station on the Up 'Flying Scotsman' on August 31, 1961: note all the trainspotters in the background enjoying the fine day. **GAVIN MORRISON**

represents the biggest improvement to the ECML in 20 years, providing 19 new services per weekday, more than three million seats per year and many faster journeys.

For the venture, Class 91 locomotive No. 91101 was reliveried in special 'Flying Scotsman' colours – complete with the iconic Gill Sans font originally introduced by the LNER in the Twenties and applied to *Flying Scotsman* the steam locomotive.

East Coast managing director Karen Boswell said: "It's part of our policy of bringing back train names and restoring pride, passion and even a touch of glamour and romance to the East Coast railway.

"It's also about listening to what our customers want.

"Many of them have asked us to bring back train naming and to provide an early morning fast express service from Edinburgh, the Borders and north east England to arrive into London well before 10am. We'll achieve both in style with our new 'Flying Scotsman'."

This time around, the named express runs only one way, south. The fastest timetabled service from London to Edinburgh now takes four hours 19 minutes.

East Coast claimed that its services have been attracting airline passengers to switch to rail, particularly from Edinburgh and Newcastle.

OTHER FAMOUS EAST COAST NAMED TRAINS

The 'Elizabethan' was a daily British Railways summer service nonstop from King's Cross to Edinburgh named to celebrate the new 'Elizabethan' era of the early Fifties. Trains departed from either end mid-morning and arrived around teatime, taking six-and-a-half hours with an average speed of just over 60mph.

LNER A4s equipped with corridor tenders were used, allowing the crew to change over while the train was in motion. The journey needed 11,000 gallons of water, so as much as possible had to be scooped up if departure from both ends was in mid-morning, for a teatime arrival.

When it was launched, it was the longest scheduled nonstop railway journey in the world.

It became the subject of a 1954 British Transport film, Elizabethan Express, which follows its journey throughout, with cinematography by Billy Williams and poetic commentary written by Paul Le Saux, and featuring No. 60017 *Silver Fox*, along with many railway staff including the Waverley stationmaster. The music score was composed by Clifton Parker, who subsequently wrote the music for the 1959 version of The Thirty Nine Steps, in which an A4 also stars.

The 'Elizabethan' last ran in September 1961. None other than *Mallard*, then numbered 60022, and based at King's Cross Top Shed, worked the Down train.

The launch of East Coast's 'Flying Scotsman' service on May 23, 2011 at Edinburgh Waverley, with power car No. 91101 painted in branded livery. **EAST COAST**

The 'Elizabethan' had replaced the 'Capitals Limited' which also ran nonstop from King's Cross to Edinburgh between 1949-53. It ceased to run in the early Sixties.

The 'Talisman' ran from King's Cross to Edinburgh Waverley from 1956-68, becoming the 'Afternoon Talisman' in 1957. A bizarre incident on the 'Talisman' occurred on December 21, 1959 when the Up service hauled by A4 No. 60012 *Commonwealth of Australia* became detached from part of its train near Morpeth. The remaining train carried on to Newcastle but the stranded coaches were shunted back into Morpeth by Gresley V2 2-6-2 No. 60865 which was transferred from a Down freight. A five-coach special for marooned passengers was run from Newcastle to King's Cross and arrived nine minutes late behind No. 60017.

A Pullman section was added during 1964-65. The train was revived in 1972-89 and extended to Aberdeen.

The 'Fair Maid' ran from King's Cross to Perth during 1957/58 and was succeeded by the 'Morning Talisman' from King's Cross to Edinburgh Waverley and Glasgow Queen Street from 1957-68.

The 'Tees-Tyne Pullman' was launched in 1948 and ran from King's Cross to Newcastle Central or Alnmouth. Apart from the 'Golden Arrow', it was the first British Pullman train to operate with a bar car, called The Hadrian Bar, which was withdrawn in 1969. The train ceased to run in 1976.

The 'Harrogate Sunday Pullman' operated between King's Cross and Harrogate and Bradford Exchange from 1927-78.

The 'Heart of Midlothian' ran from King's Cross to Edinburgh Waverley and Perth from 1951-68, while the 'Sheffield Pullman' operated between King's Cross and Sheffield from 1924-25 and 1958-68.

After 1958 the 'Master Cutler' from Sheffield Victoria, which the LNER had introduced in 1947, was switched from the Great Central route to Marylebone to King's Cross, using the ECML, diesel hauled with Pullman coaches, but after 1968 was switched to the Midland Main Line route to St Pancras.

After 2008 it started at Leeds and ran to St Pancras via Sheffield. It is regarded as Sheffield's premier business train.

The 'Scarborough Flyer' was a summer service which ran from King's Cross to Scarborough Central and Whitby Town. It was launched in 1927 as the 'Scarborough Flier' and was run as an express service from London to York, at which point the locomotive

would be changed, before the train ran on to the coast. The service continued until the outbreak of the Second World War and was revived in June 1950 as the 'Scarborough Flyer', a summer-only express. It finally ended in September 1963, but in 1981 the first heritage era 'Scarborough Spa Express' ran to celebrate the reopening of the resort's famous spa building.

The 'North Eastern' operated from King's Cross to Newcastle from 1964-68.

The 'Northern Belle' was a Pullman cruise train which ran from King's Cross to Scotland from 1933-39.

The 'Northumbrian' ran from King's Cross to Newcastle and Berwick from 1949-63.

The 'Norseman' was launched in 1948 to run from King's Cross to Newcastle Tyne Commission Quay to connect with Bergen Line or Fred Olsen Line shipping services to Norway.

The 'Yorkshire Pullman' operated from King's Cross to Bradford Exchange, Leeds, Harrogate, Newcastle or Hull from 1935-78 and 1986-88.

The 'West Riding Pullman' started running from King's Cross to Leeds and Harrogate in 1925, but was not formally named for another two years. It was extended to Newcastle in 1929 and was succeeded by the 'Yorkshire Pullman' in 1935.

With the 'West Riding' express in tow, work-stained Class A1 Pacific No. 60131 *Osprey* climbs northwards at Potters Bar on May 12, 1951. **BRIAN MORRISON**

B1 No. 1306 *Mayflower* carries the 'Yorkshire Pullman' headboard at the Doncaster Works open day in 2003. It is one of only two survivors of this once-410-strong class designed by Edward Thompson as a budget price two-cylinder mixed traffic 4-6-0, a type regularly seen on the ECML. **ROBIN JONES**

The 'White Rose' from King's Cross to Leeds Central and Bradford Exchange ran from 1949-64 and was replaced by the 'White Rose Pullman' until 1967, using carriages from the 'Queen of Scots' set.

The 'Night Scotsman' operated out of King's Cross for Edinburgh Waverley, Dundee and Fort William between 1927-87, when British Rail decided to transfer all Scotland-bound sleepers to Euston.

The 'Aberdonian' was the night sleeper service from Aberdeen to King's Cross, launched in 1927 and discontinued as a sleeper in 1972. The train itself ran until 1987.

Another sleeper train was the 'Tynesider' which ran from King's Cross to Newcastle Central from 1950-67.

The 'Car Sleeper Limited' which ran from King's Cross to Perth between 1955-66, when it was renamed Motorail, was the first train to carry cars and their passengers.

Some ECML freight trains were also named. The 'Blue Star Fish Special' began running from King's Cross to Aberdeen in 1958. Two years later, the 'Tees-Tyne Freighter' began running from King's Cross to York and Low Fell. ∎

The 'Flying Scotsman', LNER poster, 1923-1947. **NRM**

CHAPTER TEN

The day of the Deltics
...and InterCity 125s too!

Despite steam's magnificent flourish in the Fifties, its days by then were numbered. *Sir Nigel Gresley* may have set a postwar steam record on Stoke Bank, but its days in British Railways service would be numbered. Thankfully, it has been preserved, and returned to the main line to haul regular charters.

It along with five of its sisters including *Mallard* were to survive the mass withdrawal of steam, the remaining 29 members of the class ended up at the scrapyard.

Britain lagged behind other countries in announcing an end to steam haulage and switching to diesel and electric traction, a move begun in the US two decades before. Postwar austerity had the newly nationalised British Railways stick to what it knew best, steam, and under Robert Riddles, built a total of 999 new steam locomotives, the Standard classes, between 1951-60.

However, as Britain's economic situation eased and rationing ended, the national network looked to its next stage of evolution.

By the Fifties, road transport had become the biggest challenge to the railway network in its history. Just as the ECML had killed off the stagecoaches, so cars, lorries and buses now threatened the railways' survival.

British Railways understood that trains had to be made more attractive both to passengers and freight operators, by increasing speed, reliability, safety and line capacity.

On December 1, 1954, British Railways' £1240-million plan for the future was published. It was known as Modernisation and Re-Equipment of the British Railways, or the 1955 Modernisation Plan, for short.

Its headline-grabbing feature was the elimination of steam locomotives as soon as possible and their replacement with modern types of traction. It also proposed the electrification of principal main lines.

A government White Paper of 1956 claimed that modernisation would help eradicate the railways' rising financial deficit by 1962 – an aim which was far from realised, and instead led to the appointment as chairman of British Railways' cost-cutting industrialist Dr Richard Beeching, who recommended a savage series of closures of loss-making routes.

The Modernisation Plan prompted a free-for-all among locomotive designers and builders in a bid to come up with new types of diesel and electric traction. However, some types were far more successful than others: indeed, certain diesel classes hurriedly rushed into production in the Fifties barely outlived the tried-and-tested steam classes they were supposedly to replace.

The East Coast Main Line, however, became renowned for a veritable classic, in the form of the Deltic.

English Electric was a major producer of diesel and electric locomotives. Back in 1942, it had taken over engine builder D Napier &

The prototype Deltic heads through Stevenage in April 1960. **COLOUR RAIL**

The prototype Deltic DP1 outside Locomotion: The National Railway Museum at Shildon in October 2011. **ROBIN JONES**

Son on the instruction of the Ministry of Aircraft Production.

Sir George Nelson, chairman and managing director of English Electric, and his son, also George, looked into the possibility of using Napier's Deltic engine, which had previously been used in ships, to power a new type of railway locomotive.

The origins of the Deltic engine dated as far back as 1880, when the experimental Oechelhauser opposed piston scavenge blown two-stroke internal combustion gas engine was developed in Germany. The basic principles were lightness and opposed pistons, and that no heavy cylinder head was needed at one end. By 1908, the concept has evolved into

an oil fuel (diesel) compression injection engine. During the 1930s, Britain's Air Ministry had looked on the development of this type with huge interest as it was far ahead of any British diesel aero engine of the day.

After the Second World War, the Admiralty funded the further development of the type and the first Deltic Type 18.1 engine ran in April 1950. Trials were carried out in a naval vessel seized from Germany at the end of the war and they proved so successful that it was fitted inside 18 Royal Navy minesweepers.

In 1954-55, a prototype locomotive incorporating two of these Deltic engines was built at English Electric's Dick Kerr works in Preston.

Owned by its builder, it was officially numbered DP1 (Diesel Prototype No. 1) and, finished in powder blue livery with cream stripes, carried the word Deltic in large capital letters on its sides. Its distinctive front whiskers drew on the style of new American diesels, as English Electric was also thinking of the export market. A large continental-style lamp was fitted to the nose at either end.

The Magnificent Seven: the unique line-up of all seven surviving Deltics at the Locomotion museum in Shildon organised by the Deltic Preservation Society to mark the 50th anniversary of the production Class 55s. Pictured on September 7, left to right, are *The King's Own Yorkshire Light Infantry, Royal Highland Fusilier, DP1, Gordon Highlander, Alycidon, Royal Scots Grey* and *Tulyar*. **ROBIN JONES**

A row of spare Deltic Napier engines inside the Deltic Preservation Society's depot at Barrow Hill roundhouse in September 2011. **ROBIN JONES**

DP1 had a pair of 18-cylinder Napier Deltic engines (hence its name) downgraded from the 1750hp of marine engines in minesweepers to 1650hp each, reducing the stress on the engines.

The imposing blue locomotive underwent trials on the London Midland Region in October 1955, working between London and Liverpool, and also on the Settle and Carlisle line. However, officials lost interest when it became clear that the West Coast Main Line was to be electrified.

However, the Eastern Region proved more welcoming, as nobody had up to that stage come up with a blueprint for a diesel which could better Gresley's Pacifics, especially the A4s.

DP1 promised not only the power and speed the ECML required, but within the limits of a 20-ton axle load too.

It ran successfully in trials on the Eastern Region, mainly between King's Cross and Doncaster, and British Railways was so impressed that it ordered 22 production versions.

Sadly, DP1 suffered a serious powerplant failure in March 1961 and was taken out of service permanently.

Thankfully, unlike the cases of many other prototype diesels which ended up in scrapyards, DP1 was cosmetically restored and donated to the Science Museum in London, after plans to test it on Canadian railways failed to materialise. It is now part of the National Railway Museum collection and in recent years has been based at the Locomotion museum in Shildon, not too far from the ECML.

The production Deltics, which took their name from the prototype, were built between 1961-62 by English Electric and

intended to take over the ECML express trains. They were allocated to three depots: Finsbury Park in London, Gateshead and Edinburgh's Haymarket.

However, their introduction did not go smoothly, and drivers complained about several defects, which led to British Railways threatening to withdraw acceptance certificates, which meant that the maker would not get paid. Among the complaints from drivers were draughty doors which in some cases would not stay closed, slippery cab and engine room floors which quickly became contaminated with oil, and in certain cases, boiler and oil pressure switch problems. There were instances of Deltics being taken off their trains at Peterborough or Grantham and replaced by A3s, A4s or V2s.

The problems were ironed out in a relatively short space of time, and they

Spitfire Railtours ran a tour to celebrate Deltic No. 55022 *Royal Scots Grey's* 50th birthday with a trip from King's Cross to Edinburgh. It is seen approaching Tallington crossing near the start of Stoke Bank on March 5, 2011. **ROBIN JONES**

One of the prototype High Speed Train power cars has been preserved inside the National Railway Museum at York, which has been holding talks with an enthusiast group about returning it to service. **ROBIN JONES**

were delivered in a smart two-tone green, a livery which still kept one foot in the steam age. The dark British Railways green on top, with a narrower strip of a lighter, lime green along the bottom, with white for the cab window surrounds. British Railways quickly applied the bright yellow warning panel typical to diesel and electric locomotives at each end.

The Deltics were all named. The Finsbury Park locomotives took the names of winning racehorses, as per the LNER naming tradition with the A3s – after all, they were destined to be used over Stoke Bank, the steam era's greatest racetrack. However, the Deltics based at Haymarket and Gateshead took on the names of British Army regiments.

In 1964, British Railways unveiled its new corporate blue livery. Within a few years, all regional steam era liveries would disappear and be replaced by a one-size-fits-all blue or blue and white livery, which would typify the years after the last steam locomotives had been withdrawn.

Some thought that the new livery was smart; others said it was sterile. The BR blue era began in the thick of Beeching's rationalisation of the network, which saw a huge number of stations either closed or their classic infrastructure pruned back to little more than basic halts.

Deltic No. 55011 *The Royal Northumberland Fusiliers* passes Holloway on April 11, 1974. **BRIAN SHARPE**

By 1966, the Deltics started appearing in Rail Blue, as the colour was known, again with the yellow warning panels. The repaint usually came when they had additional air braking fitted, having been supplied with only vacuum braking.

With the introduction of BR's TOPS computer system for numbering locomotives and stock, the Deltics became Class 55. They were renumbered 55001 to 55022.

On the ECML, the Deltics proved themselves to be outstanding performers, and while enthusiasts hated seeing the demise of the LNER Pacifics, in time they became a type of modern traction that the steam fans might begrudgingly accept or even admire, and with good cause.

The old and the new passing at Scremerston, south of Tweedmouth, with the Northumberland coast in the background. High Speed Train set No. 254003 is heading south as Deltic No. 55010 *The King's Own Scottish Borderer* heads for Edinburgh on June 10, 1978. **GAVIN MORRISON**

Deltic No. 55012 *Crepello* lines up at York station alongside A4 No. 4468 *Mallard* on June 12, 1977. **BRIAN SHARPE**

Deltic No. 55002 *The King's Own Yorkshire Light Infantry* departs Peterborough on April 17, 1981. **BRIAN SHARPE**

Magnificent as the Deltics were, they were still very much a stop-gap in mainstream ECML traction, for the Seventies marked another sea change in British Rail stock policy.

The successful large-scale introduction of diesel railcars and multiple units in the Fifties led to the elimination of run-round loops and associated stock movements. Unlike a steam locomotive, the Ffestiniog railway double Fairlies apart, a modern main line diesel had cabs at either end, but would still need to run round its train.

That problem was eliminated with the instruction of the next stage of express trains, the Class 43 High Speed Train, branded as InterCity 125s.

While the development of its Advanced Passenger Train project was under way, British Rail decided that in the meantime it needed a new type of inter-city express train, bridging the gap between the first generation diesel multiple units and the proposed APTs.

What was produced was arguably the most successful class of passenger traction in the history of Britain's railways.

In 1970 it was decided to build two lightweight Bo-Bo locomotives to top-and-tail a rake of British Rail's new Mk3 coaches. A prototype train of seven coaches and two locomotives was completed in August 1972 and within weeks was running trials on the main line.

In May 1973, the prototype set a world diesel speed record of 143.2mph, while running on the ECML.

Three more years of trials led to British Rail's decision to build 27 production High Speed Trains for InterCity services between Paddington, Bristol, and South Wales. The first production power car, No. 43002, was delivered in late 1975, and in October 1976, a 125mph service began on the Western Region. By May 1977, the 27 units completely replaced locomotive-hauled trains on the Bristol and South Wales routes.

The King's Own Yorkshire Light Infantry, Royal Highland Fusilier, DP1, Gordon Highlander at Locomotion on October 7, 2011. **ROBIN JONES**

Until the coming of the High Speed Train, the maximum speed of British trains was limited to 100mph. Class 125s The HST were permitted a 25% increase in service speeds along many of the routes they operated. Passengers responded very favourably to their introduction.

In 1978, the High Speed Trains began replacing the Deltics on the ECML at Coast Main Line, even taking over the 'Flying Scotsman' service from King's Cross to Edinburgh from May that year.

They were concentrated on services from King's Cross to Newcastle and Edinburgh Waverley with some extending to Glasgow Queen Street, Aberdeen and Inverness, and also ran on services from London to Leeds, Bradford, Hull, Cleethorpes and Scarborough.

A world speed record for a diesel train carrying passengers was set on September 27, 1985, when a seven-car set forming a special press train for the launch of a new Tees-Tyne Pullman service from Newcastle to King's Cross reached 144mph north of York.

The record for the world's fastest diesel-powered train was set by a Class 125 unit on November 1, 1987 when it reached 148mph on the ECML during a test run for a new type of bogie later to be used under Mk4 coaches. The location? Yes, you guessed – Stoke Bank.

The type is the fastest diesel unit in the world, with an absolute maximum speed of 148mph and a regular service speed of 125mph. However, there are claims that the diesel rail speed record has been unofficially broken by a Russian train in 1992 achieving 168mph and a Spanish train hitting 158mph a decade later.

The APT project eventually withered and died in the mid-Eighties. However, the 'stop gap' Class 125s brought major improvements in services, and many of the post-privatisation Train Operating Companies, including East Coast, still have them in regular service decades on.

By 1982, when production ended, 95 High Speed Train sets including 197 Class 43 power cars had been built. To increase their life expectancy, several operators have upgraded them with the replacement of the original Paxman Valenta engines. ECML operator East Coast has continued its predecessor GNER's re-engining of the fleet with MTU engines, renumbering the power cars into the 432xx and 433xx series by adding 200 to the existing number.

High Speed Trains are likely to continue in service on the ECML until 2018, when they are scheduled to be replaced by new Hitachi Super Express units.

Meanwhile, the Deltics that they displaced in the late Seventies took on secondary duties, such as semi-fast or newspaper, parcel or sleeper services along the ECML to various destinations including branch routes to Cleethorpes, Harrogate or Scarborough. They were also used on York to Liverpool Lime Street semi-fast trains and Edinburgh to Newcastle via Carlisle stopping trains, but it soon became clear that it would be uneconomic to maintain a small non-standard class for anything other than frontline roles.

A new MTU diesel engine is carefully lowered into position on GNER HST power car No. 43120 *National Galleries of Scotland* at the Brush works in Loughborough, Leicestershire, where the engines are being fitted. **EAST COAST**

The end of the Seventies saw the first withdrawals, with the locomotives taken to Doncaster Works to be scrapped.

The last scheduled service to be worked by Deltics was the 4.30pm from Aberdeen to York on December 31, 1981. It was hauled from Edinburgh Waverley by No. 55019 *Royal Highland Fusilier*, arriving in York before midnight.

The final Deltic train of all under British Rail train was an enthusiast charter, the 'Deltic Scotsman Farewell' on January 2, 1982, from King's Cross to Edinburgh and back, hauled by No. 55015 *Tulyar* from London and No. 55022 *Royal Scots Grey* on the way back.

The Deltics had over their 20-year operational life built up an enthusiast following to the point where six were saved for preservation: D9000 (55022) *Royal Scots Grey*, D9002 (55002) *The King's Own Yorkshire Light Infantry*, which was donated to the National Railway Museum, D9009 (55009) *Alycidon*, D9015 (55015), D9016 (55016) *Gordon Highlander* and D9019 (55019) *Royal Highland Fusilier*.

The King's Own Yorkshire Light Infantry became the first preserved Deltic to make a comeback on the national network when it ran light engine to York after taking part in the Doncaster Works Open Day on February 27, 1982. It made history by being the first preserved diesel to run over the national network. It had been earmarked for preservation as early as 1980 when the Friends of the National Railway Museum sponsored a repaint into original two-tone green livery, but with full yellow ends.

Another example, *Tulyar* was even offered for sale at auction house Christie's in London by British Rail in 1982, but the reserve price of £10,000 was not met. However, it was later bought by enthusiast Peter Sansom and ended up in the possession of the Deltic Preservation Society, which was formed to save at least one Class 55 and after launching its 'The

Racehorse Appeal', was able to buy both *Alycidon* and *Royal Highland Fusilier*, which hauled the last normal revenue-earning Deltic service for British Railways.

The first of the production Deltics, *Royal Scots Grey*, was bought by the Deltic 9000 Fund, which also acquired *Gordon Highlander*, initially as a source of spares. Both are now owned by Beaver Sports (Yorkshire) Ltd and are running in their own right.

However, no Deltic hauled another train until after the privatisation of the network, which allowed open access – with anyone who had a main line certified engine able to use it.

On November 30, 1996, *Royal Scots Grey* hauled the 'Deltic Deliverance' charter from Edinburgh to Berwick. Since then, other members of the class have hauled main line charter trips.

Deltic D9015 *Tulyar* with the 'West Riding Limited' headboard at Locomotion on October 7, 2011. **ROBIN JONES**

Newly liveried National Express East Coast Class 125 High Speed Train crossing the Forth Bridge in December 2007. **EAST COAST**

In 2006, the Deltic Preservation Society brought all six production Deltic survivors together for the first time at Doncaster Works.

In April 2011, No. 55022 returned to 'real' revenue-earning service when it was hired by GB Railfreight to haul bauxite trains from Blyth to the Lynemouth aluminium smelter.

During the weekend of October 7-9, 2011, the ultimate in Deltic reunion events was staged, sponsored by Modelmaker Bachmann, to mark the 50th anniversary of the emergence of the first production examples in 1961. For the 'Golden Jubilee' of the class, the Deltic Preservation Society and the Locomotion museum at Shildon staged a one-off line-up of all seven Deltics, the six Class 55s and DP1.

THE COLLAPSE OF PENMANSHIEL TUNNEL

The ECML has continue to evolve since the end of steam, and not just in terms of traction. Indeed, several alterations to the route have been made.

One of them involved the elimination of the 800ft two-track Penmanshiel Tunnel near Grantshouse in Berwickshire, which was built to a design by John Miller, engineer of the North British Railway, in 1845/46.

There had been three major incidents in the single-bore tunnel. Firstly, the tunnel was flooded on August 12, 1948 when more than 10 inches of rain fell in a week. The waters rose to within two feet of the crown of the portal.

A year afterwards, on June 23, 1949, a fire destroyed two coaches of an express train from Edinburgh.

It is believed that the fire may have been started by a cigarette end being dropped in a corridor. The train was quickly stopped, but the fire tore through the brake composite carriage and spread to the coach in front.

Some passengers broke the windows and jumped on to the track. However, the quick-thinking crew uncoupled the four coaches immediately behind, leaving them isolated, before drawing the engine forward and detaching the blazing carriages.

The locomotive then took the front eight coaches on to Grantshouse station, as the two coaches burned down to their underframes.

There were no fatalities, but seven passengers were injured.

Far worse happened on March 17, 1979 when part of the tunnel collapsed as British Rail was widening the tunnel to allow the passage of 8t 6in containers to pass through on Freightliner wagons. The work involved lowering the track by digging out the floor of the tunnel and laying new track set on a concrete base.

The job was being done line by line, in order to minimise disruption. The Up line had been finished by March 10, 1979, before the Down line was started.

Just before 3.45am, the duty inspector saw pieces of rock flaking away from the tunnel wall, around 300ft from the southern portal. He decided to order the section to be shored up, but before he could reach the site office and give the appropriate instructions, he heard the roof crash down behind him.

Around 70ft of the tunnel arch collapsed, blocking it from floor to roof. A JCB and a dumper truck were buried in the collapse, along with their drivers.

The diversion of the ECML away from Selby eliminated the bottleneck of the swing bridge. **HARRY WILLIS/CREATIVE COMMONS**

A HM Railway Inspectorate report concluded that that the collapse was most likely to have been caused by the over-stressing of the natural rock on which the brick arch rings were founded.

However, British Rail was subsequently fined £10,000 in Edinburgh's High Court for health and safety infringements.

It was decided that repairing the tunnel would be too costly, difficult and dangerous, and so a bypass for it would be built.

Around 1100 yards of the ECML including the tunnel was therefore abandoned and a new line laid in a deep cutting built to the west. Clearly British Rail had the advantage of having modern machinery to carry out the earth moving, while back in the 19th century would have been accomplished purely by navvies using bricks and shovels.

Contractor Sir Robert McAlpine & Sons Ltd began work on the deviation on May 7, 1979 and, working 24 hours day, had it ready by August 20. During the work, part of the A1 trunk road was also realigned.

During the five months that the line was closed, trains from King's Cross ended at Berwick, with a bus link provided to take passengers to Dunbar where they rejoined the train. Other High Speed Train services to the Scottish capital were diverted from Newcastle to Carlisle and Carstairs.

Both ends of the tunnel were sealed to prevent trespass and the old line was abandoned. An obelisk was erected on the site of the collapse in memory of workers Gordon Turnbull and Peter Fowler whose bodies were never recovered, as the collapsed tunnel was not re-excavated. Today, there is little else to show where this section of one of Britain's major trunk railway routes once ran not so long ago.

Passing the 200 miles to Edinburgh sign at Benningborough is Class 47/4 No. 47412 heading an Up express to King's Cross on September 15, 1975. **GAVIN MORRISON**

Class 43 No. 43081 enters Edinburgh Waverley to form the 2.15pm to King's Cross, with No. 43089 leading, on September 24, 1981. **COLOUR RAIL**

BUILT FOR SPEED

More than four decades after *Mallard's* legendary feat, a new part of the ECML was purpose-built for speed.

In the late Seventies, the National Coal Board decided to expand its operations in the Selby Coalfield.

However, it was feared the extending mine workings would cause subsidence beneath the ECML.

As a result, the NCB paid for a new 14-mile section of railway to be built, replacing the original part of the route.

The net effect was that Selby, which in 1834 was the first railway station to open in Yorkshire, built by the Leeds & Selby Railway, was bypassed by the ECML.

Work on the new line, which cost £30-million, began on July 29, 1980, by contractor A Monks & Co. It was officially opened on October 3, 1983.

The new stretch leaves the old line at Temple Hirst to the south of Selby and rejoins it at Colton Junction several miles to the north of the town, the point where the York to Leeds line meets the ECML.

One big plus point from the scheme was that it eliminated the Selby Swing Bridge, a major bottleneck on the ECML, where four tracks had to be reduced to two.

The five-span bridge was built by the North Eastern Railway to carry the line from Leeds to Hull over the River Ouse. The swing span is 130ft long.

It also formed part of the original ECML.

The Selby diversion made history in being Britain's first purpose-built section of high-speed railway. It was designed to carry trains at speeds of up 125mph and predated the first section of High Speed 1, the Channel Tunnel Rail Link, by 20 years.

North of Selby, the old ECML was closed and in 1989 was converted into a cycle path which now forms part of route 65 of the National Cycle Network. Elsewhere, the stretch between Barlby and Riccall was taken for a new bypass for the A19.

Selby station and the southern section of the old route remains very much in use. Passenger trains run over the 'old' ECML not only to Doncaster but to London. In 2009, the town celebrated the 175th anniversary of its first station. ■

A fairly recent addition to ECML diesel power are the Class 180 five-car DMUs. The 14 units were built by Alstom between 2000 and 2001 for use on new First Great Western express services. When that company stopped using them in March 2009, they were switched to other operators. First Hull Trains Class 180 'Adelante' No. 180110 arrives at London King's Cross. **JOSHUA BROWN/CREATIVE COMMONS**

CHAPTER ELEVEN

The fastest locomotive of them all

Following the success of the electrification of the West Coast Main Line, demands arose for other trunk routes to be similarly modified.

The first part of the East Coast Main Line to be electrified was that between King's Cross and Royston, between 1975-78. As with the WCML, overhead electrification as opposed to third rail was chosen, the current being 25kV 50Hz AC.

The work was carried out as part of the Great Northern Suburban Electrification Project and also included the Hertford Loop Line, a 24-mile branch of the ECML.

In 1984, the Thatcher government gave the green light for the ECML proper to be wholly electrified, from King's Cross to Edinburgh and Leeds.

The section between Hitchin and Peterborough was completed in 1987 with Doncaster and York reached in 1989. Electrification reached Newcastle the following year and, in 1991, the last section to Edinburgh was completed.

The first electric train to call at York station. **MRM**

Also given the go-ahead was the extension of the electrification scheme on the line between Edinburgh and Carstairs, on the WCML, and the ECML's 4.7-mile North Berwick branch.

While the work was in progress, the ECML was claimed to be the world's longest construction site.

To run the new electric services, the InterCity Class 225 electric multiple units were introduced. Originally, the services were to be based around the planned new fleet of Class 89 Co-Cos, but after the InterCity 225 concept was chosen instead, and only one

Class 89, No. 89001, was ever built.

An InterCity 225 set is made of a Class 91 locomotive, nine Mk4 coaches and a Driving Van Trailer, which looks similar to the locomotive and which allows the train to be controlled from the rear.

The sets were a by-product of the aborted Advanced Passenger Train project.

The Class 91 Bo-Bos – a type named Electra – were built by British Rail Engineering Ltd., at Crewe Works while the coaches came from GEC-Alstom in Birmingham. When unveiled, the Class 91s at 6300hp were the most powerful locomotive in Britain. They

Former operator Great North Eastern Railway used Eurostar units in service on the ECML, and painted them in its livery. One is seen crossing Tallington level crossing in Lincolnshire on October 7, 2005. The original proposals for Eurostar included direct services to Paris and Brussels from cities north of London, including Glasgow via Edinburgh, Newcastle and York on the ECML. Seven shorter Eurostar Class 373/1 units for the planned Regional Eurostar services were built, but these services never ran, as in the face of low-cost airlines which could easily better the nine hours from Glasgow to Paris, they were deemed non-viable. Three of the Regional Eurostar units were leased by GNER and used on King's cross to York and Leeds services until December 2005, after which most of them were transferred to SNCF for use in northern France.

The fleeting present of Eurostars is, however, certainly in keeping with the speed traditions of the ECML. A Eurostar train set a new British speed record of 208mph on the first section of the High Speed 1 Channel Tunnel rail link on July 30 2003, and on September 20, 2007, Eurostar broke another record when it completed the journey from Brussels to St Pancras in one hour 43 minutes. **ROBIN JONES**

Officially the fastest locomotive in Britain, Class 91 No. 91110 stands at King's Cross. **MATT BUCK/CREATIVE COMMONS**

incorporated state-of-the-art computer-based electronics for power and brake control.

Among the many new features were a streamlined No. 1 end for high-speed operation, and a slab-fronted No. 2 end for slow-speed operation.

The first to be completed was No. 91001, which was unveiled on February 14, 1988, before undergoing tests from Crewe and then at the Railway Technical Centre in Derby. Test running on the ECML started from Bounds green depot in late March that year.

During a test run on, yet again, Stoke Bank, on September 17, 1989, an InterCity 225 hauled by Class 91 No. 91010, since renumbered 91110 and named *David Livingstone*, reached 162.6mph just south of Little Bytham. The DVT was leading the train.

That makes it officially the fastest British locomotive of all.

Although the Advanced Passenger Train and Eurostar units have run faster, they are both electric multiple units as opposed to locomotives.

In another test, an InterCity 225 comprised of A Class 91, five Mk4s and a DVT, covered the King's Cross to Edinburgh run in three hours 29 minutes and 30 seconds – a record for the route. The average speed was 112.5mph and the official top speed of 140mph was reached on several occasions.

The Class 91s entered passenger service on March 3, 1989 when No. 91001 hauled the 5.36pm King's Cross to Peterborough train. As the full InterCity 225 units were not ready, it comprises InterCity 125 Mk3 coaches and a Class 43 power car used as a DVT.

The locomotives entered service on King's Cross to Leeds trains with the 6.50am service on March 11, 1989, again with a makeshift arrangement of vehicles.

When it returned with the 10am from Leeds, as it was descending Stoke Bank, the guard announced that this was the spot where Mallard had set its world steam speed record of 126mph. By comparison, the Class 91 had ascended the gradient at 140mph that morning.

The full InterCity 225 units entered regular service on the ECML in 1990. However, their speed is restricted to 125mph, as regulations do not allow trains to exceed 125mph unless, as is the case with the High Speed 1 Channel Tunnel rail link, they are equipped with in-cab signalling, the reason being that lineside signals may not be correctly observed at very high speeds.

However, on June 2, 1995, an InterCity 225 set what was then a new UK record for a passenger train when it reached 154mph on a Newcastle to Peterborough service.

A total of 31 Class 91s were built, the last being delivered in February 1991.

Electrification work on the ECML in progress. **NRM**

The unique Class 89 locomotive No. 89001. Built by BREL Crewe during 1985-87, after extensive tests it was transferred to the ECML and Hornsey and Bounds Green depots. It was used in service until May 1988 when it was sent to Hamburg along with a Class 90 and a Class 91 power car and a two-car Class 150/2 DMU. It returned to the ECML and worked until 1990 when it was taken out of service due to technical defects. It was preserved at the Midland Railway-Butterley in 1992, but was bought by Great North Eastern Railway which returned it to Bounds Green. It began hauling King's Cross to Leeds and Bradford in place of a Class 91, but again suffered problems. In 2006, it was again bought by preservationists, this time in the form of the AC Locomotive Group, which would like to return it to serve. **ROBIN JONES**

Major refurbishment of the class began at Adtranz Bombardier Doncaster in 2000, with Alstom overhauling the internal equipment. The driving cab interiors were modified to provide the driver with more information.

*For the record, on July 30, 2003, on the first press run of High Speed 1, the Channel Tunnel rail link, Eurostar unit No. 3313/14 set a new British rail speed record of 208mph, breaking the previous record of 161.2mph set by an Advanced Passenger Train on December 20, 1979.

THE 'RENATIONALISATION' OF THE ECML

Services on the ECML became the first part of the network to be taken back into state control when, in early November 2009, the government took over the East Coast franchise.

National Express had run the franchise since 2007, when it had won it with a £1.4 billion bid, but decided to hand the contract back after the government refused cash aid to its National Express East Coast subsidiary. The company had tried to renegotiate the

terms of the contract but talks broke down as the government became worried that other private rail companies, also suffering from a drop in passenger numbers, would want similar help.

The Department for Transport set up Directly Operated Railways Limited as an operator of last resort after the franchise was handed back, effectively renationalising the franchise. East Coast Main Line Company Ltd., was established as a subsidiary of directly Operated Railways, with the trading name of East Coast.

All 3100 National Express staff transferred to East Coast from midnight on November 13, 2007. The trains were also eventually reliveried.

On August 5, 2011 Secretary of State for Transport Philip Hammond announced that the new Inter City East Coast franchise would commence in December 2013. Until then at least, East Coast would continue to run the services to Edinburgh, Leeds and Yorkshire.

The previous operator before National Express, Great North Eastern Railway, handed back the franchise in 2006 after

revenue receipts were far lower than expected and the company found that it was unable to meet the £1.3 billion in premium payments it had promised the Government in return for the franchise. One reason given was that the July 7, 2005 terrorist attacks in London led to a major fall in tourism in the capital.

Today, the ECML is said to carry 17 million passengers a year.

THE EAST COAST MAIN LINE TODAY

Legendary, yes. Perfect, no.

The upsurge in passenger traffic since the late Eighties has more than justified the decision not to downgrade or close the section of the route north of Newcastle.

However, there remain bottlenecks, where the number of tracks reduces to two, and which will continue to impede the further growth of traffic until they are relieved.

Not only is there to aforementioned Welwyn Viaduct, but it remains part of a four-mile two-track section on one of the busiest parts of the route, the other pinch point here being the Welwyn tunnels.

A Class 91 East Coast service caught in a snowstorm at Doncaster on December 2, 2010. **EAST COAST**

A Class 225 unit at King's Cross headed by DVT No. 82208 carries the East Coast livery. **ROBIN JONES**

The future of the East Coast Main Line: Southeastern 'Javelin' unit No. 395002 departs St Pancras with a preview service to Ebbsfleet International in 2010. **MATT BUCK/CREATIVE COMMONS**

Ancient and modern: A4 Pacific No. 60019 *Bittern* heads south towards King's Cross with a railtour as an InterCity 225 unit headed by Class 91 No. 91132 heads in the opposite direction into Peterborough station. **BRIAN SHARPE**

At nearby Hitchin, trains from King's Cross running on or off the line to Cambridge have to cross three other tracks on the grade at a flat junction. The flat crossing at Newark is also viewed as a problem, while there is another two-track section at Stilton Fen between Peterborough and Huntingdon. Also, Doncaster has difficulties with regard to the number of branch trains that it can accept on its Up platform.

Otherwise, the ECML has mainly four tracks from King's Cross to Stoke Tunnel, south of Grantham. There are also four-track sections at Retford and Doncaster, between Colton Junction (south of York), Thirsk and Northallerton, and at Newcastle.

Only the line between Leeds Neville Hill Depot and Colton Junction is not electrified.

Aided by large tracts of flat land on the edge of East Anglia, most of the line is passed for 125mph running: indeed, it was officially the fastest main line in the UK until High Speed 1 was opened.

Many proposals have been made to improve the ECML. They include the building of a grade-separated junction to the north of Hitchin in order to allow Down Cambridge trains to cross the main line.

One frequent criticism is that the electrification was done 'on the cheap', hence wires and masts occasionally failing in very high winds. Power supply upgrades including improvements to the overhead supply supports and rewiring have been called for.

It has been suggested that the Welwyn section could be made into four tracks by boring two extra tunnels and carrying the railway over the viaduct in double-deck fashion.

Full reversible signalling over the Stilton Fen section, replacing the Newark flat crossing with a flyover and increasing the line speed from 125mph to 140mph, when the new Hitachi 'Javelin Trains' replace the existing stock. Indeed, a manufacturing facility for the new trains has been pencilled in for a site in Newton Aycliffe, County Durham.

Another idea is to link the ECML to the Thameslink tunnels which already provide a north-south route across the city from St Pancras next door. That would allow First Capital connect, which runs commuter trains from Peterborough and Cambridge to King's Cross, to take them on to south London.

One recent development has been the building of the Allington Chord near Grantham in 2006, allowing services between Nottingham and Skegness to pass beneath the ECML.

This improvement alone allowed 12 extra daily services between King's Cross and Leeds, so think of the benefits that every one of the suggested improvements could also bring. ■

Wearing LMS postwar lined black livery, LMS Princess Coronation Pacific No. 6233 *Duchess of Sutherland* heading the 'Coronation' on May 17, 2010 passes an East Coast Class 91 travelling in the opposite direction on the ECML. While the heritage era regularly sees locomotives running on routes that they would never have tackled in steam days, there is some historical precedence for this. In the 1948 Locomotive Trials, when the newly-formed British Railways decided to experiment with locomotives inherited from the 'Big Four' companies being used on routes for which they had not been specifically designed, sister locomotive No. 46236 *City of Bradford* did some runs on the ECML, hauling the King's Cross-Leeds express. **PA KING / CREATIVE COMMONS**

Class 91 No. 91132 *City of Durham* heads a GNER service northwards past Werrington on the outskirts of Peterborough.

No. 91132 (then 91023) was involved in the Hatfield rail crash on October 17, 2000, in which its GNER InterCity 225 King's Cross-Leeds train was travelling at around 115mph when it derailed south of Hatfield station, due to the left-hand rail fracturing as the train passed over it. The accident left four passengers (all in the restaurant car, which overturned onto its side and struck an overhead line gantry) dead and injured a further 70.

Little more than four months later, just after 6am on February 28, 2001, it was propelling an InterCity 225 train when it was involved in the Great Heck rail crash, in which 10 people were killed and 82 people suffered serious injuries. A Land Rover Defender towing a loaded trailer swerved off the M62 just before a railway bridge. The vehicle ran down an embankment and on to the southbound railway track. Its driver was Gary Neil Hart, who the jury was told had fallen asleep at the wheel after spending the previous night on the telephone talking to a woman he had contacted via an internet dating agency. Hart attempted to reverse the vehicle off the track, but he could not. While he was using his mobile telephone to call the emergency services, the vehicle was struck by the southbound GNER service heading from Newcastle to King's Cross at over 120mph.

The leading bogie of the DVT derailed but the train stayed upright, only for it to be directed by points to nearby sidings and straight into the path of an oncoming Freightliner train from Immingham to Ferrybridge hauled by a Class 66 diesel locomotive. This second crash occurred about half a mile from the first. Before this second impact, the speed of the GNER service was estimated as 88mph and that of the freight train as 54mph. The estimated combined speed of 142mph made the crash the highest speed railway incident in British railway history.

Both train drivers, two additional train crew on board the 225, and six passengers died. Hart was found guilty on 10 charges of causing death by dangerous driving and on December 13, 2001 was sentenced to five years' imprisonment. He was released after serving half his sentence. **BRIAN SHARPE**

The DVT of an InterCity 225 after arriving at King's Cross through a snowstorm on December 21, 2009 stands alongside an East Coast Class 125 unit. **ROBIN JONES**

CHAPTER TWELVE

Closure beyond Newcastle?

The East Coast Main Line is nothing short of a national treasure. Not only are the many speed records set on the route a great reason for national pride, but it performs the workaday function of linking two capital cities 393 miles apart.

So it may, therefore, come as a surprise to modern readers that there have been attempts to downgrade or even close part of it.

The name Dr Richard Beeching is a household word for railway closures, and while he has his critics, he also has supporters, who believe that not only did he streamline a process of rail closures that had already been under way for many years but pruned the national network into a slimmer, fitter beast in which it was able to compete with road transport – by this day the A1 Great North Road was well into its ascendancy again – but reshape rail transport so it could face future challenges, whatever they were.

However, while his 1963 report, the Reshaping of British Railways, was a seminal point in British transport history, much less well known was his follow-up report in February 1965. Nicknamed 'Beeching II', the report highlighted trunk routes that would justify large-scale investment to handle projected increases in both passenger and freight traffic over the next two decades. That in itself seemed fair enough, but critics immediately said that the routes that had not been listed would face closure.

One of these routes was the Newcastle to Edinburgh line. Had it been terminated at Newcastle, northbound trains would have been rerouted to Carlisle, from which, following the controversial closure of the Waverley Route, only one route would have been left to link London with Scotland.

Beeching denied that the routes not listed for development were under threat, saying: "For the sake of clarity, it is emphasised that non-selection of lines for intensive development does not necessarily mean that they will be abandoned in the foreseeable future, nor even that money will not be spent upon some of them to improve their suitability for their continuing purpose." Despite this many were not convinced, and breathed a sigh of relief when he left British

Railways shortly afterwards, returning to his original post at ICI.

The report identified the ECML from King's Cross to Newcastle as the future primary route for traffic between London and the East Midlands, South Yorkshire and the Tyne-Tees area, but rejected the alternative through Cambridge, March, Spalding, Lincoln and Doncaster, part of which was the original GNR main line.

The threat did not go away with Beeching, however.

In 1982, the lowest number of passenger journeys of the second half of the 20th century was recorded on the network, while car ownership was at an all-time high. The passenger deficit was £933-million, and with costs continuing to rise, it was inevitable that the Margaret Thatcher government would eventually consider drastic steps.

A committee chaired by Sir David Serpell KCB CMG OBE, a senior civil servant who had worked under Dr Beeching, looked at the worsening problem of the railway's deficit.

In his report, Railway Finances, published in January 1983, Serpell went further than Beeching had ever dared to go.

One option contained in it was the reduction of the network's 10,370 route miles down to 'bare bones' of just 1630 profit-making miles.

It would have left London-Bristol/Cardiff, London-Birmingham-Liverpool/Manchester-Glasgow/Edinburgh, and London-Leeds/Newcastle as the only main lines left. Some London commuter lines would remain, but all others would close.

The popular British Rail chairman from 1976-83, Sir Peter Parker, said that he found Serpell "as cosy as a razor blade".

Mainly because of the report's extremely harsh first option, it provoked so much outrage that it was quickly shelved, and it led to no changes being made to the network.

However, it gave an insight into the way that some in the corridors of power were thinking.

As it was, passenger numbers improved from then on, reaching a 20-year high in 1988, and with privatisation looming in 1993, Serpell's report was forgotten.

Thankfully, the magnificent section of the ECML built by the North British Railway is still open and flourishing.

May it long stay that way! ■

RAILWAY FINANCES, PUBLISHED IN JANUARY 1983, SERPELL WENT FURTHER THAN BEECHING HAD EVER DARED TO GO.

Two Virgin Cross Country Voyager units head northwards past Burnmouth, the first village in Scotland on the A1, en route to Edinburgh, on July 7, 2006. The North British Railway main line from Edinburgh to Newcastle could have been closed under one option outlined in the Serpell Report in 1982. **BRIAN SHARPE**

CHAPTER THIRTEEN

The steam speed legends today

The greatest monument to the legacy of the East Coast Main Line stands alongside it. The National Railway Museum, which is housed in one of the former York North shed roundhouses, and offers a grandstand view of the main line from one of its viewing galleries, is home to three of the greatest steam legends of all time – *Mallard*, *City of Truro* and *Flying Scotsman*.

Having a collection of more than 100 locomotives and nearly 200 other items of rolling stock, it was opened on a 20 acre site in 1975, replacing the Clapham Transport Museum in London which had housed items from the National Collection, and the York Railway Museum which had been established by the LNER. The museum was opened by the Duke of Edinburgh as the 150th anniversary celebrations of the opening of the Stockton & Darlington Railway – a constituent of the North Eastern Railway – were taking place.

Among its many honours is the European Museum of the Year Award 2001, and it attracts more visitors than any other British museum outside London.

When you first walk into its Great Hall, it is easy to see why it's so popular. So many 'greats' from the days of steam and pioneer diesel and electrics are displayed in pristine condition, as if new out of the box, from a replica of Stephenson's *Rocket* to a Japanese Bullet Train. It is like a *Boys Own* book of trains literally coming alive, and there is more in Station Hall, the former depots' good shed. Since 2001, admission has been free, as is the case at the museum's outstation, Locomotion: The National Railway Museum at Shildon.

One of the first exhibits that greeted visitors for many years was none other than the world's fastest steam locomotive, *Mallard*. It is only fitting that the locomotive which marks the pinnacle of the entire steam age should have pride of place in what many critics have described as the best railway museum in the world.

MALLARD

Built at Doncaster in 1938, *Mallard* remained in service until April 25, 1963.

In 1948, the newly-nationalised British Railways tested the best locomotives from the 'Big Four' companies to find the best attributes of speed, power and efficiency with coal and water. One of the aims was to draw up new designs for the planned Standard series of locomotives, of which 999 were eventually built.

The express passenger locomotive designs which would be compared were the LMS Princess Coronation class, the A4s, the Southern Region Merchant Navy class and the Western Region's Kings.

The three A4s that took part were *Mallard*, given the number E22, No. 60033 *Seagull* and No. 60034 *Lord Faringdon*, all fitted with the Kylchap double blastpipe chimney arrangement and fresh out of Doncaster Works, *Mallard* having received its fourth boiler and third tender and a new livery, post-war garter blue, with stainless steel numbers.

On June 8, 1948, *Mallard* ran on the Waterloo-Exeter route. Despite being held back by a succession of red signals, its train was only 5½ minutes late, and at Axminster it had reached 82mph. Sadly, *Mallard* failed after the run and was replaced by *Seagull*.

Mallard returned to the Waterloo-Exeter line for a Locomotive Club of Great Britain railtour on February 24, 1963.

During its career, *Mallard* was allocated to three sheds: Doncaster as new, Grantham on October 21, 1943 and King's Cross on April 11, 1948.

The liveries carried by *Mallard* had included garter blue as No. 4468, changing to LNER wartime black from June 13, 1942, later wartime black with the tender marked as NE from October 21, 1943, as E22 with yellow small stencilled numbers, post-war garter blue with white and red lining from March 5, 1948 with stainless steel cabside number 22, British Railways dark blue as 60022 from September 16, 1949, Brunswick green from July 4, 1952 and repainted in its first livery after being preserved.

Like the other 34 A4s, *Mallard* was fitted with streamlined valances when built. This side skirting was removed to ease maintenance in wartime, but *Mallard* regained it when preserved.

In preservation, *Mallard* has only a fleeting main line career. Its last appearance was on August 27, 1988, running from Eaglescliffe to Newcastle, Carlisle and back to York. It is seen at Birkett Common on the Settle & Carlisle line, shortly before stalling due to a spark arrestor becoming clogged with ash. **BRIAN SHARPE**

Mallard back at Doncaster in 2003 for an open weekend at 'The Plant'. **ROBIN JONES**

During its 25 years in traffic, *Mallard* had 12 boilers and seven tenders, beginning with a non-corridor version and ending when recoupled to the same to recreate its 1938 appearance.

When finally withdrawn from King's Cross by British Railways, it had covered nearly 1.5 million miles. It became part of the National Collection because of its steam feat, commemorated by plaques fixed to each side of the locomotive, and immediately moved to its Doncaster Works birthplace for cosmetic restoration.

The engine entered Clapham Museum on February 29, 1964, and was towed to the NRM on April 12, 1975.

The NRM returned it to working order in the Eighties, and it ran its first heritage era main line railtour on July 9, 1986, when it ran from York to Scarborough and back via Hull and Goole.

On July 3, 1988, *Mallard* lined up at the NRM with two other preserved A4s, No. 4498 *Sir Nigel Gresley* and No. 60019 *Bittern*,

which the year before had been cosmetically restored as No. 2509 *Silver Link*, which, thanks to intransigence at the Eastern Region at the time, astonishingly was not saved.

Mallard steamed for the last time on August 27, 1988, and has since then remained a static museum exhibit.

On the weekend of July 5, 2008, *Mallard* was taken outside for the first time in years and displayed alongside three fellow A4 sisters, the abovementioned two, with *Bittern* by now long back in its original identity, and No. 60009 *Union of South Africa,* which had been bought by enthusiast John Cameron in 1967.

On June 23, 2010, *Mallard* was towed to the Locomotion museum for static display, returning by rail on July 19, 2011. After a reshuffle of locomotives in the Great Hall, from October 12, 2011, it was positioned alongside LMS Princess Coronation Pacific No. 6233 *Duchess of Hamilton,* one of its streamlined rivals from what was arguably the greatest decade of steam.

SIR NIGEL GRESLEY

As with the other members of the 35-strong class, *Sir Nigel Gresley* wore many liveries throughout its career. It was released to traffic on October 30, 1937 in the standard LNER garter blue of the A4 Pacifics. New numbers and letters for the tender in stainless steel were added in a general overhaul January 16, 1939. *Sir Nigel Gresley* was repainted into wartime black with LNER markings on February 21, 1942. The next repaint was into black with NE markings on October 20, 1943, as a cutback. After the war, *Sir Nigel Gresley* regained LNER garter blue livery with red/white lining on March 6, 1947. With the formation of British Railways came new liveries and the engine was painted into British Railways dark blue with black and white lining on September 27, 1950. The final livery change was into British Railways Brunswick green livery on April 17, 1952. In preservation *Sir Nigel Gresley* wore garter blue (with stainless steel letters and numbers as 4498 added later) from 1966 until overhaul

A4 Pacifics No. 4498 *Sir Nigel Gresley*, No. 60019 *Bittern* as No. 2509 *Silver Link* and No. 4468 *Mallard* at the National Railway Museum in York on July 3, 1988, the 50th anniversary of *Mallard's* record run. **BRIAN SHARPE**

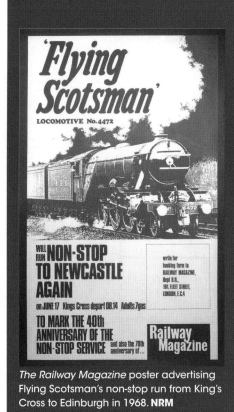

The Railway Magazine poster advertising Flying Scotsman's non-stop run from King's Cross to Edinburgh in 1968. **NRM**

in the late 1990s, when it gained its current British Railways blue livery as No. 60007. This livery was retained again after the 2006 overhaul.

THE A4 WITH 12 BOILERS

As with the earlier LNER A4 Pacifics, *Sir Nigel Gresley* was built with single chimney and side valances covering the wheels. The valances were removed to aid in maintenance on February 21, 1942. The engine gained its double chimney and Kylchap double

blastpipe on December 13, 1957. 60007 also gained AWS (Automatic Warning System) equipment on September 27, 1950. A Smith-Stone type speed recorder was fitted on June 30, 1960.

Sir Nigel Gresley has had 12 boilers in its career: 8961 (from new); 8946 (from 4483 *Kingfisher*), February 21, 1942; 9489 (new boiler), March 6, 1947; 29271 (from 60024 *Kingfisher*), September 27, 1950; 29319 (new build), April 17, 1952; 29306 (spare), October 19, 1953; 29321 (from 60010

Dominion of Canada), March 12, 1955; 29314 (from 60026 *Miles Beevor*), April 13, 1957; 29324 (from 60015 *Quicksilver*), December 13, 1957; 29331 (new build), April 16, 1959; 27970 (new build), October 7, 1960 and finally 27966 (from 60016 *Silver King*), October 25, 1962.

Sir Nigel Gresley had two tenders in its career: 5329 from new build to August 8, 1943 and then 5324 from that time.

Fifty years to the day that A4 Pacific No. 60007 *Sir Nigel Gresley* set the post-war record for steam traction at 112mph, on May 23, 2009 it was back on the East Coast Main Line with the York to King's Cross 'Golden Jubilee' and is seen passing the famous flat crossing at Newark. **BRIAN SHARPE**

CAREER

Outshopped by the LNER in October 1937, and the 100th Gresley Pacific built, A4 No. 4498 had been due to receive the name *Bittern*, originally suggested for No. 4492 (later *Dominion of New Zealand*). It is said that a member of the Railway Correspondence &Travel Society who worked for the LNER realised in time that No. 4498 was the 100th Gresley Pacific and suggested that it be named after its designer. The name *Bittern* was later carried on No. 4464.

As new, No. 4468 *Sir Nigel Gresley* was allocated to King's Cross from new, moving to Grantham in April 1944 but returning to Top Shed in June 1950.

The locomotive also featured in the opening of British Railways' Rugby testing station from August 23 to October 8, 1948. Placed on a set of rollers minus its tender, it was run up to high speeds to monitor its coal and water consumption.

After the King's Cross shed closed, the locomotive, then No. 60007, moved to New England shed on June 16, 1963.

Another move to St Margarets shed, from which it hauled to Edinburgh-Aberdeen trains, was followed by its last shed allocation, to Aberdeen on July 20, 1964.

It was withdrawn by British Railways on February 1, 1966. A group of enthusiasts began efforts to save it under the banner of the A4 Preservation Society – quickly renamed the A4 Locomotive Society – to prevent it from being scrapped.

After the group bought the locomotive, it was moved to Crewe Works for overhaul, and while there it was given the six driving wheels from sister A4 No. 60026 *Miles Beevor* because they were in far better condition.

After the Carnforth steam shed closed, it became a heritage railway museum called Steamtown. From there, once British Rail had relaxed its 1968 steam ban, *Sir Nigel Gresley* ran main line railtours.

Now based at the North Yorkshire Moors Railway, Britain's most popular heritage line, it is in daily operation following a 10-year overhaul to working order. It is owned by the Sir Nigel Gresley Locomotive Preservation Trust Ltd and operated by the A4 Locomotive Society Ltd.

UNION OF SOUTH AFRICA

Outshopped from Doncaster in late June 1937 and originally named *Osprey*, No. 60009 *Union of South Africa* saw its first name was revived in the Eighties and early Nineties due to public disgust over the apartheid policies of the country whose name it carried.

The springbok plaque on the side of the locomotive was donated on April 12, 1954 by a Bloemfontein newspaper proprietor.

The locomotive had a double chimney fitted on November 18, 1958, a type first fitted to *Mallard* in 1938.

When built, 'No. 9' as the engine is popularly known, was allocated to Haymarket shed in Edinburgh. On May 20, 1962, it was switched to Aberdeen.

Union of South Africa made history by hauling the last booked steam-hauled train from King's Cross on October 24, 1964.

It was also the last steam locomotive overhauled at Doncaster Works while in service.

Withdrawal came on June 1, 1966, after which it was sold into preservation. New owner and Scottish farmer John Cameron for

many years had his own line on which to run it, the Lochty Private Railway in Fife.

His Lochty Farm included the final three quarters of a mile of a 15 mile freight-only branch running from East Fife Central Junction between Leven and Cameron Bridge.

In 1967 he relaid the track on the formation through the farm and erected an engine shed to house *Union of South Africa* which, following preservation, had worked the last steam special in Scotland in 1967.

The A4 was steamed every Sunday afternoon, a member of the record-breaking class of Gresley streamlined East Coast Pacifics now carrying passengers at very slow speeds over a remote short private line.

Following the end of the British Rail steam ban, in January 1973 two routes were allocated in Scotland for the running of steam special trains. *Union of South Africa* carried the first such special, on May 5 that year, and hauled its nine-coach trains at speeds of up to 60mph over the Edinburgh to Dundee main line.

With The A4 back on the main line, alternative steam power was obtained for the Lochty Private Railway, but it closed in 1992. Support organisation the Fife Railway Preservation Group became the Kingdom of Fife Railway Preservation Society and moved its stock from Lochty to sites in nearby Methil, where it has bought a 20 acre site which it aims to open as a railway heritage centre.

On October 29, 1994, it appropriately hauled the first steam out of King's Cross for 30 years on a railtour to Peterborough, under the banner of the 'Elizabethan', making more ECML history, or rather carrying on from where it had left off in 1964.

LNER A4 4-6-2 No. 60009 *Union of South Africa* heads north past Eggborough power station towards Temple Hirst Junction near Selby with a tour from King's Cross to York on December 2, 2006. **BRIAN SHARPE**

No. 60009 is now a regular main line tour performer and has now accumulated the highest mileage of any A4.

BITTERN

Built at Doncaster and outshopped on December 18, 1937, from new *Bittern* was based at Heaton in Newcastle. It hauled the 'Flying Scotsman' between King's Cross and Newcastle, and after the Second World War, the 'Talisman' from London to Edinburgh.

Originally numbered 4464, *Bittern* became No. 60019 under British Railways.

Its last sheds were St Margarets, to which it was transferred on October 28, 1963, and

Ferryhill at Aberdeen from November 10, 1963, from where it ran to Edinburgh and Glasgow. Indeed, it was the last A4 to haul the Glasgow to Aberdeen service.

It was withdrawn on September 3, 1966, and bought by Geoff Drury on September 12 that year. It was then moved to York North and from there ran railtours in the final days of British Rail steam.

However, when bought it had badly-cracked frames and its Indian summer back on the main line soon came to an end. Geoff Drury then switched his attention to Peppercorn A2 No. 60532 *Blue Peter* and bought it from British Rail in 1968.

Both found a new home at the now-closed Dinting Railway Centre near Glossop in Derbyshire and were looked after by the North Eastern Locomotive Preservation Group.

While *Blue Peter* found its way back on to the national network, *Bittern* was cosmetically restored as the far more famous No. 2509 *Silver Link*, as mentioned above.

Eventually, *Bittern* was bought by pharmaceuticals entrepreneur Dr Tony Marchington, who sold it on to multi-millionaire enthusiast Jeremy Hosking in January 2001. He moved it to Ropley Works on the Mid-Hants Railway where serious restoration work began.

LNER A4 Pacific No. 60019 *Bittern* in its new guise as No. 4498 *Dominion of New Zealand* passes Aycliffe in County Durham with the Railway Touring Company's 'Great Britain IV' on April 16, 2011. **DEE DAVISON**

Bittern steamed for the first time since the Seventies on May 19, 2007, outshopped in British Railways Brunswick green and hauling services on the heritage line. Following test runs, *Bittern* made its revenue-earning comeback on the national network on December 1, 2007 on a charter from King's Cross to York.

Unlike the other surviving A4s, *Bittern* has had only one tender throughout its career. Starting out as a non-corridor type, it was rebuilt as a corridor type during the engine's last major overhaul in 2007, to boost flexibility of operation of railtours.

A second tender was coupled to *Bittern* on July 25, 2009, allowing it to run all 188 miles from London to York non-stop. It carried a 'Brighton Belle' headboard to draw attention to the 5BEL Trust's groundbreaking restoration of a five-car 'Brighton Belle' EMU set, Britain's only electric Pullman train, and which has been supported by Jeremy Hosking.

In 2011, *Heritage Railway* magazine exclusively revealed that Jeremy Hosking had ordered *Bittern* to receive another identity exchange, becoming No. 4492 *Dominion of New Zealand*, with valances refitted and the repainting of the locomotive into LNER garter blue with the wheels in their original red colouring, and steel lettering and numbers on the sides. *Dominion of New Zealand* had, like *Union of South Africa*, been one of five A4s named after Commonwealth countries to pull the Coronation, which marked the accession of George VI in 1937. It is due to remain as No. 4492 for three years.

LNER A4 Pacific No. 60019 *Bittern* storms through Stukeley north of Huntingdon on the ECML. **BRIAN SHARPE**

FLYING SCOTSMAN

As we have seen, Gresley A3 Pacific No. 4472 acquired fame not only for hauling its namesake train in eight hours non-stop from King's Cross to Edinburgh from 1928, but also for its official 100mph record six years later.

However, its many adventures during the preservation era have enhanced its standing as the world's most famous steam locomotive.

On January 4, 1947, its conversion from an original A1 into an A3 was completed, receiving a boiler with the long banjo dome of the type it carries today.

It spent two periods in the Fifties not on the ECML but working the one-time rival Great Central route. Based at Leicester Central shed, it hauled Nottingham Victoria to Marylebone services in the era when the route was being run down and eventually closed. It was eventually transferred back to King's Cross.

British Railways had the A3 Pacifics fitted with double Kylchap chimneys to improve both performance and economy. The result was that soft exhaust and smoke drift obscured the driver's forward vision, so from 1960, German-style smoke deflectors were fitted, solving the problem.

East Coast meets West Coast: on October 12 2011, *Mallard* was positioned alongside the turntable in the Great Hall at the National Railway Museum, next to LMS Stanier streamlined Princess Coronation Pacific No. 6229 *Duchess of Hamilton*, representative of the type which rivalled the A4s on the alternative route from London to Scotland in the golden age of steam of the 1930s. **BRIAN SHARPE**

Flying Scotsman at the US National Railroad Museum at Green Bay, Wisconsin, in 1969, before the North American tour went bust. **A WAPPAT/NRM**

Former *Flying Scotsman* owners Alan Pegler (seated) and Sir William McAlpine (far right) at the unveiling of *Flying Scotsman* at York on May 27, 2011. **KIPPA MATTHEWS/NRM**

The world's first railway to be taken over by volunteers was the Talyllyn Railway, where preservation era services began in 1951. Shortly afterwards, businessman and former dive-bomber pilot Alan Pegler spearheaded the rebirth of the Festiniog Railway as a heritage line, with a volunteer-led group taking it over and beginning restoration in 1954.

Alan Pegler then moved up from narrow gauge locomotives to full-size Pacifics, when he bought *Flying Scotsman*, then carrying its British Railways number 60103, following its withdrawal in January 1963. He had always held affection for *Flying Scotsman* after seeing it at the British Empire Exhibition all those years before.

It remains today a matter for great astonishment that it was not earmarked for public preservation as part of the National Collection, and could so easily have ended up in a scrapyard. A fund had been launched under the banner of Save our Scotsman but when it failed to reach the £3000 asking price, Alan Pegler stepped in and bought it himself.

In 1964, sister locomotive No. 60106 headed the 'Flying Scotsman' train at King's Cross after a Deltic had broken down: it would be the last time that a steam locomotive would haul the famous named train.

Alan Pegler had *Flying Scotsman* restored at Doncaster Works as closely as possible to its LNER condition. The 'modern' smoke deflectors were removed, the double chimney was replaced by a single chimney, and the tender was exchanged for a corridor version of the type coupled to the locomotive from 1928-36. It was also repainted into LNER apple green, which has become its trademark livery.

Flying Scotsman's first outing in private ownership was laid on for Ffesiniog Railway Society members in April 1963, taking them to their annual general meeting.

The locomotive was provided with a second tender in 1966, to allow it to carry extra water at a time of great change when steam facilities such as water columns were being ripped out in the cause of modernisation.

On May 1, 1968, *Flying Scotsman* recreated the steam-hauled non-stop run from King's Cross to Edinburgh, as tens of thousands of people watched from the lineside. The feat would never be repeated.

When British Rail banned steam haulage after August 11, 1968, when the last steam railtour, the '15 Guinea Special' ran, one exception was made – *Flying Scotsman*, which was permitted to run on the main line until 1972.

Pegler saw that the powers that be on the main line did not want steam, and so looked further afield for a new stomping ground for *Flying Scotsman*, and came up with the idea of a tour of North America to promote British businesses.

Following overhaul in the winter of 1968/69, the A3 was fitted with a US-style cowcatcher, bell, buckeye couplings, American-style whistle, air brakes and high-intensity headlamp. Comprising a train of Pullman cars and steam era coaches, the train carried trade stands for 21 of the UK's largest exporting firms. Alan Pegler paid for a British Rail locomotive crew to drive *Flying Scotsman* and the trip received the backing of Labour Prime Minister Harold Wilson.

Flying Scotsman's 60th birthday outings saw steam return to the ECML for the first time since 1969, and comprised three Sunday trips from Peterborough, beginning on February 27, 1983, two of them to York and the third to Carnforth. No. 4472 became reacquainted with Stoke Bank and is seen bursting forth from the north portal of Stoke Tunnel. At the time there was hardly a blade of grass around the tunnel mouth: today, this scene is totally inaccessible as it is heavily wooded and overgrown. **BRIAN SHARPE**

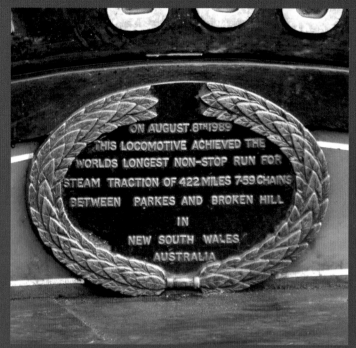

The plaque commemorating the world record non-stop steam run in Australia remains on No. 4472's middle driving wheel splasher.

Taking the ECML down under: *Flying Scotsman* on its first Australian railtour, from Melbourne to Albury. **BRIAN SHARPE**

At first, the trip was a success, although the train was fired at by IRA sympathisers when approaching New York. The tour covered more than 2200 miles and visited 17 US states in 1969.

The following year, another tour was planned, and proud Pegler had been given dispensation by the US authorities to drive the locomotive himself. However, the financial backers pulled out. Nonetheless, the train ran from Texas to Toronto.

Money by now had run out, and with the accounts very much in the red, Alan Pegler took the train 3000 miles to 'British Week' in San Francisco in a bid to clear his debts. It did no such thing: the train was marooned in California, No. 4472 moved to an army base for safekeeping, and Pegler, by then bankrupt, was forced to work his passage back to Britain as a ship's entertainer.

Concern was expressed that No. 4472 could be left permanently in the US, or even be cut up. Alan Bloom, founder of Bressingham Steam Museum in Norfolk, telephoned multi-millionaire enthusiast Sir William McAlpine and informed him of the A3's plight.

Sir William McAlpine sent George Hinchcliffe, the ill-fated tour manager, to the US to arrange a rescue package, and then bought the locomotive for £25,000 direct from the finance company in San Francisco docks.

It returned to the UK via the Panama Canal in February 1973, and was repaired at Derby Works. When it ran under its own steam from Liverpool to Derby, around 100,000 people turned out to welcome it home. Trial runs took place on the Paignton & Dartmouth Steam Railway that summer, after which it was transferred to Steamtown at Carnforth, from where it hauled several railtours, including one in 1984 along the North Woolwich branch in East London, with the Queen Mother on board.

In 1988, Sir William McAlpine accepted an invitation to send No. 4472 to take part in the Australian bicentennial celebrations, and it arrived in Sydney that October.

During 1989, it entertained huge crowds as it travelled across the country, making a transcontinental run from Sydney to Perth, and also became the first standard gauge steam locomotive to run to Alice Springs.

On August 8 that year, it travelled 442 miles from Parkes to Broken Hill non-stop, the longest run of its type ever recorded by a steam locomotive. A plaque on the engine commemorates the event.

While in Australia, No. 4472 met up with GWR 4-6-0 No. 4079 *Pendennis Castle*, which had beaten *Flying Scotsman* in the 1925 Locomotive Exchanges, and which McAlpine had sold to an Australian mining company. *Pendennis Castle* was repatriated in 1999 and is being restored to main line running order by the Great Western Society at Didcot Railway Centre.

Flying Scotsman returned to Britain in early 1990, after 15 months away. Its journey around Cape Horn meant that it had sailed around the globe.

MacAlpine then joined forces with former BR worker Pete Waterman, who had made his fortune as a pop producer. Together they formed Flying Scotsman Railways, to take advantage of the open access policy offered by rail privatisation under the Margaret Thatcher Tory government. It did not work out, and the locomotive was sold in 1996 to the abovementioned Dr Tony Marchington in a bid to clear its debts.

There followed a three-year restoration under the auspices of engineer Roland Kennington at Southall Railway Centre in West London. After a few late-night test runs in grey primer, No. 4472 made a triumphant return to the East Coast Main Line on July 4, 1999. An estimated one million people turned

Former owner Dr Tony Marchington with the locomotive that he restored to the main line in 1999. **ROBIN JONES**

out to watch it run from King's Cross to York.

Again, No. 4472 was to prove a financial millstone. Dr Marchington set up an operating company and in 2001 sold shares in it, allowing the public to buy their own stake in No. 4472 for the first time, and then made plans for a 'Flying Scotsman Village' theme park, first at Ambergate in Derbyshire and then at Edinburgh, but they came to nothing. The company was failing to cover its costs.

The company's annual accounts for the year ending December 31, 2002 showed a loss of £474,619 for the year: for every pound the locomotive earned, the cost of just running its owning company, excluding the repairs and maintenance, was £1.87.

In February 2004, *Heritage Railway* magazine revealed the A3 was being offered for sale… by a car dealer.

Vintage, veteran and classic car specialist Malcolm C Elder & Son had been inviting bids for No. 4472 after claiming that it had "been asked to discreetly market the world's most famous steam locomotive."

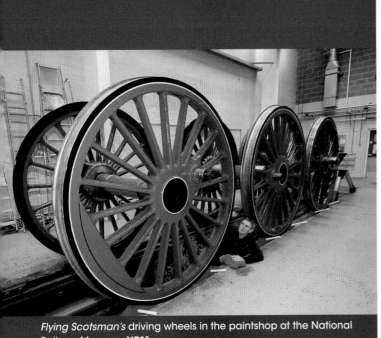

Flying Scotsman's driving wheels in the paintshop at the National Railway Museum. **NRM**

Flying Scotsman arrives at York station following its £2.31 million purchase for the nation. **NRM**

Shortly afterwards, Flying Scotsman plc offered the locomotive for sale.

The National Railway Museum led the race to buy it. An appeal was launched, with Sir Richard Branson offering to match money raised by the public. The National Heritage Memorial Fund also provided financial support, and amid fears that the A3 could be sold abroad, the purchase price of £2.31 million was raised. The sale was announced on April 5 that year, and shortly afterwards, Flying Scotsman, serenaded by bagpipes, arrived at the NRM at the start of Railfest 2004, an event which marked the 200th anniversary of the first public demonstration of a steam locomotive, by Richard Trevithick.

Finally, 41 years after being sold to a private individual, Flying Scotsman was owned by the nation again. Alan Pegler was among those who witnessed the public handover ceremony.

In late 2005, Flying Scotsman entered the museum's workshops for a major overhaul to main line running standard, and an appeal was launched for funds. The public responded again and contributed around £250,000.

A decision was taken to repair the worn A3 boiler acquired with the locomotive as a spare, and sell the A4 boiler it had used since the early 1980s to Jeremy Hosking for use on Bittern. The boiler was subsequently repaired at Ian Riley's engineering works at Bury.

The overhaul, however, was beset by delays and Flying Scotsman, the world's most famous locomotive, became the most expensive one too.

On May 27, 2011, the world's press joined VIPs at a high-profile relaunch of Flying Scotsman, which had been painted into wartime austerity black livery as No. 502. former owners Sir William McAlpine and Alan Pegler were among the crowd.

The plan afterwards was to take the locomotive back to Ian Riley's workshop for fettling prior to test runs on the East Lancashire Railway, main line tests and then a public repainting into LNER apple green at the museum that August.

Flying Scotsman unveiled to the public in the Great Hall of the National Railway Museum on May 27, 2011. However, it later transpired that all was still not well with the A3, and its target for a return to the main line was delayed until late spring 2012. **ROBIN JONES**

GWR unofficial record breaker 4-4-0 No. 3717 *City of Truro* was donated to the LNER museum at York in 1931. It is seen in action on the Bodmin & Wenford Railway on September 2, 2011. **BERNARD MILLS/BWR**

It did not happen. Back at the workshops, what looked like a harmless hair from a paintbrush on one of the hornguides was noticed. An attempt was made to scrape it off, but then it was discovered that it was not a brush hair, but a crack. A subsequent examination found cracks in other hornguides. Furthermore, problems with other components came to light, including rectification work needed on the six driving wheels. Also, a new mid-stretcher, axle box machinations and a new middle motion bracket were needed.

On September 30, 2011, museum director Steve Davies held a press briefing at Bury. He revealed that the cost of the overhaul had topped £2 million and would rise further. Parent body the National Museum of Science and Industry had agreed to divert resources from other projects to finance the extra work, he said.

He also said that a formal internal investigation into why the overhaul had cost so much money, both from public funds and private donations, and why it had taken so long, was underway. The investigation would examine the project management since the overhaul began in 2005, he said.

Nonetheless, he said the aim was to have No. 4472 present at a landmark line-up of East Coast motive power. In May 2012, there is scheduled to be an A1, A2, A3 and A4 stand shoulder-to-shoulder at Barrow Hill roundhouse near Chesterfield.

Steve Davies added that the locomotive would probably steam again in late spring 2012, running at first in wartime black, before being taken into the Great Hall at the museum and repainted into LNER apple green.

Finally, he revealed that the A3 had been booked to carry the Olympic flame for the

London 2012 games over part of its route. And so the legend lives on.

CITY OF TRURO

GWR 4-4-0 No. 3440 (later 3717) *City of Truro* is not a locomotive that was associated with the ECML in its working life.

However, the LNER led the way in recognising railway heritage when, in 1927, it opened a public railway museum in York.

In March 1931, *City of Truro*, which had run in daily service since its alleged 102.3mph feat in 1904, was withdrawn. Great Western Railway chief mechanical engineer Charles Collett asked for it to go the York museum after his company's directors refused to fund the cost of preserving it.

Donated to the LNER, it was despatched to York from Swindon on March 20, 1931, and it became a popular exhibit a stone's throw from the ECML.

During the Second World War it was moved to the small locomotive shed at Sprouston station near Kelso to protect it from bomb damage.

Surprisingly, British Railways returned it to service in 1957, as No. 3440: it was used not only for special railtours, but in everyday service on the Southampton to Newbury line.

Withdrawn again in 1961, it was preserved in Swindon's GWR Museum the following year.

Part of the National Collection, it was restored to running order in time for the GWR 150 celebrations in 1985, and was afterwards based at the National Railway Museum from where it ran occasional tours. It was subsequently restored in 2004 so that it could again run over Wellington Bank where it was said to have broken the 100mph barrier in 1904. It has been based at the Gloucestershire Warwickshire Railway and also visited other heritage lines.

In 2010, to mark the 17th anniversary of the GWR, it was repainted into its correct livery as No. 3717. At the time of writing, it is on static display in The Locomotion museum following the discovery of serious boiler tube leaks. ∎

National Railway Museum director Steve Davies with the frames of *Flying Scotsman* at Bury on September 30, 2011. The boiler had been lifted while further rectification work took place. **ROBIN JONES**

CHAPTER FOURTEEN

East Coast steam: the legend storms on!

The record-breaking days of steam on the East Coast Main Line are all but certainly over. At the time of writing it is inconceivable that any steam locomotive will ever be given the chance to better *Mallard's* world record set on Stoke Bank.

Since British Rail relaxed its 1968 ban on further main line steam hauled trains three years later, several classic locomotives have again graced the route of the 'Flying Scotsman'.

However, modern speed restrictions on steam locomotives mean that they can travel at no more than 75mph. And with an absence of steam infrastructure such as water columns, or better still water troughs, for express trains on the move, long journeys on the ECML necessitate periodic stops rather than nonstop running.

The preservation era saw *Flying Scotsman* enhance its reputation as the world's most famous steam locomotive.

Yet while it was away undergoing a long-running overhaul at the National Railway Museum, it faced a serious challenge to its crown, from a brand new locomotive that, as far as the general public at large was concerned, appeared from nowhere as if to steal its thunder.

It was new Peppercorn A1 Pacific No. 60163 *Tornado*, built from scratch by a group formed by a handful of enthusiasts in 1991 at a cost of £3-million.

In April 1990, enthusiast Mike Wilson of Stockton-on-Tees, lamenting the failure to save the last A1, No. 60145 *Saint Mungo*, for preservation in 1966, proposed in the now-defunct fortnightly newspaper

Recreating an ECML scenario on the North Yorkshire Moors Railway, Britain's most popular heritage line, is *Tornado* in British Railways apple green livery carrying a 'Flying Scotsman' headboard and departing from Goathland with a set of LNER teak coaches. **DON BRUNDELL/A1SLT**

Steam Railway News that a group should be set up to build a new Peppercorn Pacific.

Reading his words were the Champion brothers David and Phil. David had been looking at the idea of new-built since the Sixties.

He had seen engineer Mike Satow's Locomotion Enterprises outfit's building of a working replica of Stephenson's *Rocket* in 1979 and the Ffestiniog Railway's new double Fairlie *Earl of Merioneth* appear the same year.

These may be considered small alongside a main line Pacific. However, enthusiasts who bought part-sectioned Unique British Railways Class 8P Pacific No. 71000 *Duke of Gloucester* from Woodham Brothers'

scrapyard at Barry – and had not only restored it but implemented modifications which improved its steaming – it was possible to make many new components. Logically, therefore, it would be possible to build a new standard gauge locomotive, even though no production line or erecting shop survived from the steam era.

Needless to say, there were many who said that it could not be achieved. However, there is no stopping the enthusiast sector once it believes something can be done.

From the outset, there were many who said it couldn't be done. However, initial pure enthusiasm for the recreation of a much-

Tornado crosses the famous flat crossing at Newark-on-Trent with a southbound railtour. **BRIAN SHARPE**

In Brunswick green livery, *Tornado* approaches Newark with the King's Cross to York 'Cathedrals Express' on August 13, 2011. **GEOFF GRIFFITHS/A1SLT**

loved postwar express passenger locomotive type won the day.

The Champion brothers wrote to Mike offering to join the project, and David recruited heritage steam locomotive engineer Ian Storey and Newcastle-upon-Tyne lawyer Stuart Palmer. The five launched the project in York at the end of 1990, after the National Railway Museum confirmed that all the A1 drawings still existed.

David saw that it was insufficient to build a replica A1 Pacific. Their locomotive had to be the next A1 Pacific, the 50th member of the class. That would legitimately allow minor changes to be made to Arthur Peppercorn's original design to meet modern standards. It would take the next number after No. 60162 *Saint Johnstoun*, the last in sequence of the original class.

One of the big reasons why the project was successful was the fact that the founders realised that enthusiasm would not be enough. Money was the answer, and finding ways of raising large amounts of funds was equally as important as carrying out exhaustive research or making the first components.

David produced a scheme whereby supporters would sign up to donate the price of a pint of beer a week.

Tornado at Gamston Bank with 'The Talisman' on February 7, 2009. It was the day when No. 60163 ran into King's Cross for the first time, with a charter from Darlington. **ALAN WEAVER/A1SLT**

No. 60163 hauling the BBC Top Gear special 'Cathedrals Express' charter northbound through Doncaster. **DAVID COOPER/A1SLT**

Six days after the four launched The A1 Steam Locomotive Trust, 120 people attended the inaugural meeting at the Railway Institute in York on November 17, 1990. So great was the attendance that people were standing on the stairs outside. David himself signed the first covenant to donate money regularly, and within 30 minutes, 100 people had also signed up, while several top quality professional people came on board – Barry Wilson, then vice-president of Bank of America in Jersey, Wreford Voge, an accountant and expert on charities from Edinburgh, aero industry engineer David Elliott and marketing man Mike Fanning from Doncaster.

Two years later, marketing expert and future A1 Trust chairman Mark Allatt was recruited, to be joined by experienced project planner Rob Morland and then Andrew Dow, the previous head of the National Railway Museum.

Four years later, the first and last components, a bogie swivel pin and a regulator nut, were unveiled. On April 22,

A1 Pacific No 60163 *Tornado* heads the 25 April 2009 King's Cross-Edinburgh 'The Cathedrals Express' through Peterborough on the centre road. **BRIAN SHARPE**

1994, building began with the rolling of the frame plates at Scunthorpe.

It was decided to call the new locomotive *Tornado*, after the RAF fighter bomber which featured in the First Gulf War. The following January, the nameplates were presented by officers of the Royal Air Force at the frame laying ceremony at Tyseley, and also that year, the first wheel was cast.

The project was initially based at Tyseley Locomotive Works in Birmingham under the auspices of chief engineer Bob Meanley. It was there that three cylinder castings were unveiled in May 1997.

In March 1997, the frame was displayed at the Great Hall at the National Railway Museum, while that year the project moved to the former Hopetown Carriage Works next to Darlington North Road station. The building accordingly became a new Darlington Locomotive Works.

By 2000, half of the building was complete, and in 2004, it had become a rolling chassis. The biggest job of all was the

boiler, and after failing to find a British manufacturer, and more finance became available through commercial loans, a contract was placed with Dampflokomotiv Meiningen, workshops which had been part of the former East German railway system which had continued with steam engineering.

In June 2007, the boiler and firebox assembly were fitted to the frames, and on January 9, 2008, *Tornado* was pushed by locomotive out of the works into the sunshine after a fire had been lit in its boiler.

Tornado was publicly unveiled to the media outside the Darlington works on August 1, moving up and down on its short length of track, and wearing grey primer as its livery.

A few days later, *Tornado* as taken by road to the Great Central Railway at Loughborough, Britain's only double track heritage trunk railway, which in BR days was a rival to the ECML, for running in. It was there, on September 21 that it hauled its first passenger train, and afterwards, moved to The National Railway Museum at York from

where main line test runs began on November 4, No. 60163 still carrying the grey undercoat. The third and final main line test run was completed on November 19.

It was on December 13 that *Tornado* appeared in its first livery, British Railways apple green, the LNER corporate colours with 'British Railways' in large lettering on the tender. Prior to *Tornado*, Thompson B1 No. 1306 *Mayflower* and LNER D49 No. 246 *Morayshire* were the only two operational steam locomotives painted in apple green. LNER V2 No. 4771 *Green Arrow* was withdrawn from main line operations on April 26, 2008 by owner the National Railway Museum. Apple green was also the last livery carried by *Flying Scotsman* before it was withdrawn in December 2005.

Tornado's ECML pedigree was reinforced by the fact that its smokebox door also carries the identification plate 51 A, the code for Darlington shed. The cab side carries the builder's plate No. 2195 Darlington 2008.

The new A1 exiting Hadley Wood Tunnel with 'The Talisman' on February 7, 2009. **GEOFF GRIFFITHS/A1SLT**

On January 31, 2009, spectators filled every viewpoint alongside the ECML from York to Newcastle-upon-Tyne to watch *Tornado* pull its first passenger train, 'The Peppercorn Pioneer.' A week later, on February 7, *Tornado* ran into King's Cross for the first time, hauling 'The Talisman' from Darlington.

On February 19 that year, at York station on the ECML, *Tornado* received its highest accolade of all. It was officially named by Prince Charles and the Duchess of Cornwall before hauling the Royal Train to Leeds. The prince donned a boiler suit and rode on the footplate.

Among the proudest people on the York platform that day was Mrs Dorothy Mather, the trust's president and the widow of designer Arthur H. Peppercorn who died 56 years before. On February 28, No. 60163 made it first journey up the ECML into Scotland with 'The Auld Reekie Express' from York to Edinburgh, and on March 7, it became the first A1 out of Edinburgh for 40 years, hauling the 'North Briton' back to York.

On April 18, it became the first A1 to run out of King's Cross for 40 years.

The locomotive recalled the days of the Great North Road, latterly the A1, in a unique stunt for BBC's Top Gear motoring show amid tight secrecy on Saturday, April 25.

The 10-coach private charter from King's Cross to Edinburgh might, *Tornado* apart, have seemed little out of the ordinary, but Top Gear presenter Jeremy Clarkson was on the footplate acting as fireman.

The locomotive, representing a design from the late Forties, was racing two vehicles from the same period, from London to Edinburgh. Top Gear colleagues James May was driving a Jaguar XK120 and Richard Hammond a Vincent Black Shadow motorbike, both on the old A1. They were not allowed to use motorways as they had not been built back in the Forties. A helicopter was booked to fly overhead the train to capture all the action.

Tornado should have won. However, due to delays entering Waverley station, the steam train came second and the motorbike third. Nonetheless, *Tornado* kept to its booked time of eight hours, which included water stops at Grantham, York, Newcastle and Berwick – effectively 6½ hours by steam

age standards – the whole affair was screened on June 21, 2009.

By then, the whole nation had woken up to the fact that Britain could build main line express locomotives again: *Tornado* was the first new steam locomotive to appear on the national network since British Railways outshopped Standard 9F 2-10-0 No. 92220 *Evening Star* at Swindon in 1960. It seemed that everyone, captivated by a flurry of newspaper headlines, wanted to see the shiny new beast for themselves, whether or not they had previously shown any interest in railway heritage. Everywhere *Tornado* went, the crowds followed, packing out station platforms.

Its first venture over the spectacular Settle and Carlisle route came on October 3-4, 2009 and its first run over Shap summit on the West Coast Main Line followed a week later.

On December 21, *Tornado* hauled a Steam Dreams Christmas special from Waterloo around Kent to Dover and back. Again, nothing special in that – but the weather was atrocious – so bad in fact that the wrong type of snow meant that the modern-day diesel multiple units used to provide commuter

Tornado prepares to depart from Newcastle with the return leg of its first-ever main line passenger-carrying trip, 'The Peppercorn Pioneer' on January 31, 2009. **ROBIN JONES**

Still in grey primer, *Tornado* hauls its first passenger train, on the Great Central Railway on September 21, 2008. **ROBIN JONES**

services could not run.

However, the wintry weather presented no problem for a veteran ECML steam design. Thanks to *Tornado*, marooned Kent commuters hopped on board the steam special to get home.

Tornado again hauled the Royal Train with Prince Charles and the Duchess of Cornwall on board on February 4, 2010, to the Museum of Science & Industry in Manchester.

Two days later at York, the Heritage Railway Association presented The A1 Steam Locomotive Trust with its highest accolade, the Peter Manisty Award, in recognition of its unique accomplishment in raising the profile of the British railway heritage movement to the general public and throughout the world. Still more was to come. *Tornado* beat the previous record for the fastest steam-hauled railtour over Shap summit by 19 seconds, on June 24, 2010.

The A1 Trust had always intended to paint No. 60163 in all the liveries that the first 49 A1s carried during British Railways days. Brunswick green, the livery remembered by most, was the top choice for enthusiasts.

Accordingly, *Tornado* appeared in pre-1957 Brunswick green with the initial BR lion and wheel symbol for the first time at the NRM on February 9, 2011. The liveries yet to come are post-1957 Brunswick green and the short-lived BR express passenger blue.

On September 21, 2010, *Tornado* hauled the longest public steam day excursion since 1968, all 505 miles from Crewe via Manchester, Shap and Beattock to Glasgow, over the 'rival' West Coast Main Line, and back via Wigan.

In theory, *Tornado* is capable of reaching 100mph, but that would not be allowed under current Network Rail restrictions. However, at some stage, it may be given permission to do 90mph, making it the fastest steam locomotive on the British national network. If that happened, any such run would more likely than not take place on the greatest steam race track of all, the East Coast Main Line, and there surely would be standing room only along the whole of its length, as another proud chapter in its history was written. The races to the north will never be forgotten.

The A1 Steam Locomotive Trust is now planning to follow up its achievement by building a Gresley P2 Mikado. ∎

Prince Charles officially names *Tornado* at York station on February 4, 2009, watched by proud A1 Trust chairman Mark Allatt. **ROBIN JONES**

CHAPTER FIFTEEN

Wizard times at King's Cross

Flying Scotsman has often been described as the world's most famous steam locomotive. Yet its international fame, particularly on the East Coast Main Line, was eclipsed in the 21st century by a far more humble Great Western Railway Hall class 4-6-0 that otherwise had no historical connection with the route.

It may have travelled far and wide, but its fame has been eclipsed on a global scale by a GWR Hall – one that no longer appears in Brunswick green. Also an ex-Barry wreck, it was restored to main line condition by owner David Smith, who runs Carnforth-based train operating company West Coast Railways, and in 1997 made a trial run over Shap at the beginning of its comeback.

No. 5972 Olton Hall was outshopped from Swindon in April 1937 and was first allocated to Neath shed in South Wales, being transferred to Carmarthen 13 years later. After that came a move to Plymouth Laira.

Named after a mansion in Solihull, Olton Hall was withdrawn from Cardiff East Dock shed in December 1963 and sent to Woodham Brothers' famous scrapyard at Barry, the 'steam Valhalla'.

In May 1981, it became the 125th out of 213 steam engines sold by Dai Woodham for preservation when it was acquired for restoration by Procor (UK) Ltd in Wakefield. It was subsequently acquired by David Smith, owner of Train Operating Company West Coast Railways, which restored it to main line condition at its Cardiff base.

Throughout its working life, Olton Hall carried GWR Brunswick green livery and

was just one of 259 members of the class of honest reliable mixed traffic locomotives.

However, everything changed when in 2001 West Coast painted it a decidedly non-authentic bright red, and suddenly it became the engine that everyone wanted to see.

West Coast signed a deal with Warner Brothers to produce a locomotive that would star in the big-screen movie version of J K Rowling's Harry Potter books.

Olton Hall fitted the part. It was renamed Hogwarts Castle, after the fictional train in the books, and a rake of West Coast British Railways Mk1 maroon coaches was provided to make up the 'Hogwarts Express'.

In its film role, the locomotive carries a 'Hogwarts Express' headboard on the smokebox, featuring the Hogwarts School crest. The same emblem is featured as part of the Hogwarts Railways' emblem on the tender and carriages.

In the film, the locomotive retains GWR number 5972, but has Hogwarts Castle nameplates replacing the Olton Hall ones.

Much location filming was undertaken at King's Cross using the 'Hogwarts Express' train, which arrived, of course, via the ECML.

Platform 4 was used for the secret Platform 9¾, which only wizards can see. Trains packed with extras stood at Platforms 3 and 5 during the filming.

The real platforms 9 and 10 are located in the 'commuter' station on the west side, but J K Rowling intended Platform 9¾ to be inside the original Lewis Cubitt-designed part of the station. The film follows her wishes in this respect.

Afterwards, a Platform 9¾ sign was erected on a wall near the platform. It became one of London's most popular (and free) tourist attractions.

With the refurbishment of King's Cross in recent years, the Platform 9¾ sign has been moved to an enclave in the wall immediately to the east of the entrance to the King's Cross station complex. It seems that every day, visitors are forever queuing up there to have their pictures taken beneath the sign.

A Hornby OO gauge model of Hogwarts Castle has proved so popular that it has been one of the manufacturer's biggest sellers in recent years, especially before Christmas, and train sets have been produced to coincide with the release of new Harry Potter films. However, the Hornby model is based on the GWR Castle class locomotive, not a Hall.

When not used for filming, the locomotive hauls special excursions over the national network. It can often be seen at the National Railway Museum next to York station.

The terminus, Hogsmeade, is in real life Goathland on the North Yorkshire Moors Railway. The railway shop became the prefects' room and the ladies' loos became the wizards' room. The West Highland Extension between Fort William and Mallaig with its spectacular Glenfinnan viaduct has also been used for film sequences involving the train.

In 2010, a full-size and amazingly accurate wooden mock-up of Hogwarts Castle appeared at the new Wizarding World of Harry Potter theme park in Orlando, Florida.

The Harry Potter movies are not the first time that King's Cross has been used for major location filming. Many scenes of the 1955 movie The Ladykillers starring Alec Guinness and Herbert Lom were filmed there.

The stolen money in The Ladykillers is hidden in a parcel delivered on a train from Cambridge hauled by a GNR N2 0-6-2 tank engine. Much of the film action takes place around Copenhagen tunnel. ∎

A daily sight outside King's Cross in 2011 was regular queues of Harry Potter fans waiting to have their picture taken beneath the Platform 9¾ sign, which has been temporarily moved outside the station while building work is in progress. **ROBIN JONES**

Hogwarts Castle aka Olton Hall on display at Doncaster Works open day in 2003. **ROBIN JONES**

Hogwarts Castle waits at the head of the 'Hogwarts Express' on Platform 9¾ at King's Cross in 2006. **DALE SMALLIN**

CHAPTER SIXTEEN

Termini
for the future

Aerial view of King's Cross and neighbour St Pancras International, showing some of the building work under way. **NETWORK RAIL**

Both East Coast Main Line termini have been undergoing major redevelopment schemes to ensure that they can cope with the ever-increasing demands of a third century of passenger travel by rail.

In 2005, a £500 million restoration plan for King's Cross was announced by Network Rail. The plan is based on a six-year restoration of the arched roof of the station and the demolition of the 1972 extension, which will be replaced by an open-air plaza, and will allow Lewis Cubitt's magnificent façade of 1852 to be fully seen again.

In addition, a semi-circular concourse is being built on the west side of the station to replace the existing shopping area and East Coast ticket office, providing greater integration between the intercity and suburban sections of the station. The new 8,000 square metre concourse is three times the size of the existing one.

A new open space bigger than Leicester Square will be created in front of the station when the present concourse is removed.

As part of the scheme, a new platform 0 opened on the east side of the station on May 20, 2010, in the space formerly occupied by a taxi rank. It was built to minimise disruption during restoration when some of the other platforms would be temporarily out of use, although it has also fulfilled the need to increase capacity.

When the refurbishment is complete, all the platforms will be renumbered, the new one becoming platform 1.

Also, the 885ft-long Grade I listed iron and glass roof above platforms 1 to 8 is being completely refurbished, with 7500 clear glass panels and more than 1400 photovoltaic panels, which will reduce the station's carbon footprint by 10%, replacing the yellowing 1970s glass fibre. On September 19, 2011, passengers could pass through the concourse at King's Cross station bathed in natural daylight for the first time in half a century after the first section of the new roof was unveiled.

English Heritage and conservation planners have been closely involved in all aspects of the restoration, which combines traditional materials and techniques with 21st-century engineering and building technology not available to Cubitt.

Most of the station redevelopment, including a new concourse to the west of the station, is scheduled to be completed in time for the 2012 Olympic Games, with the rest completed by 2013.

The new station will include integrated transport links with St Pancras International and the London Underground. Once the scheme is completed, the station will be able to accommodate 50 million passengers a year, 10-million more than before.

To the north of the station, the King's Cross Central regeneration scheme aims to remove the area's tarnished image forever. The 67-acre development includes shops and offices, 1,900 new homes, 20 new streets, 10 new major public spaces and the restoration of 20 historic buildings and structures.

A view of the 'new' King's Cross trainshed roof from the central platforms.
NETWORK RAIL

What King's Cross station will look like once the existing concourse is removed to show the original façade which will be restored. **NETWORK RAIL**

Computer visualisation of the new King's Cross showing the western concourse.
FACADE REVEALED

It is hoped that the refurbishment of King's Cross will be as successful as that of St Pancras, when it was significantly altered to handle trains on high Speed 1 from the Channel Tunnel, with its heritage features preserved intact and even enhanced.

Meanwhile, 393 miles to the north, Edinburgh Waverley, which today has around 23 million passengers a year, is having its 34,000 square metre roof replaced, as part of a £130-million refurbishment of the station.

The scheme involves the installation of 28,000 clear glass panels, flooding the station with natural light. There will also be new fully accessible entrances from Market Street and from Princes Street via Waverley Steps.

The station concourse will also be resurfaced and station building exteriors given a facelift. The project was scheduled for completion by summer 2012.

In June 2011, Network rail unveiled a blueprint for a major enhancement of Leeds station. The plans include a new entrance and concourse on the south side of the station, a better choice of shops and restaurants on the north concourse, improvements to the New Station Street entrance and 350 extra car parking spaces for passengers.

Artist's impression of the new southern entrance to Leeds station.
NETWORK RAIL

Artist's impression of the new King's Cross western concourse.
NETWORK RAIL

The existing King's Cross concourse and front entrance as seen in September 2011. **ROBIN JONES**

Fitting new glazing panels in the roof of Edinburgh Waverley Station. **NETWORK RAIL**

An aerial view of Waverley station looking east towards Arthur's Seat. **NETWORK RAIL**

Passenger numbers in Leeds are set to rise by 16% by 2014 and by 62% by 2029.

A £2.5-million upgrade for Peterborough station, a popular starting point for London commuters, was announced by Network rail in January 2011.

The entire station will be transformed with a smart new frontage outside and a brighter interior. Under the plans, the size of the concourse will be increased, with more seating, a new waiting room and automatic ticket gating. ∎

A section of the new 15,000 square metre roof as soon from above. **NETWORK RAIL**

The planned new entrance to Peterborough station. **NETWORK RAIL**

CHAPTER SEVENTEEN

Six of the best

The streamlined A4 Pacific is a definitive icon of British achievement, an epitome of the great age of steam. It is therefore surprising that not more than the six examples which exist today were saved from the cutter's torch.

Four of them are resident in Britain, while two, No. 60008 *Dwight D. Eisenhower*, and No. 60010 *Dominion of Canada*, have permanent homes in North America. When withdrawn from main line service, they found new homes at the National Railroad Museum in Green Bay, Wisconsin, and Exporail, the Canadian Railway Museum in Montreal respectively. If not for that, they might also have been scrapped.

It has been said that No. 60012 *Commonwealth of Australia* was similarly offered to the Australians, but the transport costs proved prohibitive, and it was instead scrapped.

For many years, enthusiasts have speculated that one day, one or both of the A4s across the Atlantic might return home. However, their museum owners have repeatedly rebuffed requests for repatriation or to sell them.

However, in August 2011, *Heritage Railway* magazine exclusively reported that moves were underway to reunite all surviving A4s, for a unique line-up at the National Railway Museum in 2013.

The magazine discovered that senior NRM staff had been undertaking top-secret detailed planning to borrow Nos. 60008/10 for the line-up, which would mark the 75th anniversary of *Mallard's* world record-breaking run on Stoke Bank in 1938.

By the time the story was published, the NRM confidential talks had been held between the NRM and its counterparts in the US and Canada for six months.

Agreement was reached between the NRM and the North American museums, but with very strict conditions attached.

Both museums will allow the locomotives to 'take a holiday' in the UK, perhaps for a year or more, provided that the transport was shown to be feasible, and on the understanding that both will return to North America when the temporary loan period ends. Some cosmetic restoration to *Dominion of Canada* would be carried out as part of the deal.

Moveright International haulier Andrew Goodman, a market leading expert in international locomotive shipping, made two trips to both North American museums on behalf of the NRM. While in the US, he also undertook the repatriation of exiled Sharp Stewart 0-4-4T *Dunrobin*, which arrived back in May 2011 and is destined for a new permanent home at Beamish Museum in County Durham.

He was asked by the NRM to see whether it was possible to physically move the locomotives out of the buildings in which they are housed and transport them to the nearest port, and indications were that it was indeed possible.

The locomotives are likely to be taken to Halifax by Canadian National and loaded on to a cargo ship there.

If the proposed line-up goes ahead, it stands to be one of the biggest achievements in both the history of the preservation movement and its centrepiece, the NRM, since it was opened by the Duke of Edinburgh in 1975.

No. 60008 *Dwight D. Eisenhower* on display at Green Bay, Wisconsin. **DAVE RODGERS**

Heritage Railway's view of what the planned line-up of six A4 Pacifics could look like.

No. 60010 *Dominion of Canada* pauses at Doncaster with an Up express in June 1962. **COLOUR-RAIL.COM**

The big task is to find the funding to move both locomotives to the UK and back again. Rough estimates gave a figure of £400,000. It was likely that a public appeal might be launched as well as major sponsorship sought.

NRM director Steve Davies said: "I cannot emphasise strongly enough that this is a loan proposal and will emphatically not result in the permanent repatriation of either or both of these locomotives. This has been explicit in our negotiations from the outset and I am most grateful that our colleagues in the US and Canada have so far shared this exciting vision with us."

In the 1950s, as steam disappeared from US railroads earlier than in Britain, a National Railroad Museum was established in Green Bay, Wisconsin, by the Great Lakes, west of Chicago.

A chance conversation between a lady called Mrs Kovachek, who was on holiday from Yorkshire, and a man she thought was the gardener, resulted in the first of the pair going to North America.

The 'gardener' turned out to be the chairman of the museum's board, Harold E Fuller. When he found out that there was a

IF THE PROPOSED LINE-UP GOES AHEAD, IT STANDS TO BE ONE OF THE BIGGEST ACHIEVEMENTS IN BOTH THE HISTORY OF THE PRESERVATION MOVEMENT AND ITS CENTREPIECE, THE NRM SINCE IT WAS OPENED BY THE DUKE OF EDINBURGH IN 1975

locomotive named *Dwight D. Eisenhower* in the UK, he became determined to add it to the collection.

British Railways, however, would not sell it to him. The LNER's No. 4496 *Golden Shuttle* had been renamed after the US war hero and later president, but in the late 1950s was still hard at work on BR expresses.

General Eisenhower had strong connections with Britain's railways as there had been two military command trains in Britain during the run-up to D-Day, which were for the general's exclusive use. These trains, mainly of GWR stock and codenamed 'Alive', did include two LNER Gresley coaches, which were the general's favourites.

When No. 60008 was withdrawn, along with several of the King's Cross allocation, in 1963, BR was happy to donate the engine and the two LNER coaches used by General Eisenhower, to the Green Bay museum. There they were displayed together for many years from 1964.

It was only in recent years that research on both sides of the Atlantic has led its US custodians to realise that *Dwight D. Eisenhower* would almost certainly never have hauled either of its namesake's military trains in Britain during the Second World War.

Still in BR green livery, as restored at Doncaster prior to export, the A4 in 2000 was given pride of place in a new museum building at Green Bay, still with the Gresley coaches attached, and standing alongside Union Pacific articulated 4-8-8-4 'Big-Boy' No. 4017. The idea is that a member of the world's fastest class of steam engines stands next to the world's biggest.

Subsequently, a National Railroad Museum was also set up in Canada, and with No. 60008 already donated for preservation in the US, British Railways could hardly refuse a request from the Canadian museum in Montreal for No. 60010 *Dominion of Canada*.

No. 4489 was one of the early batches of A4s that carried apple green livery and the name *Woodcock*. A batch of A4s received Commonwealth names and garter blue livery, for working the LNER 'Coronation' and 'West Riding Limited' expresses, and No. 4489 was renamed *Dominion of Canada* and repainted garter blue within two weeks of entering service, becoming No. 60010 in BR days. It was withdrawn in 1965, having been transferred to Scotland to work the Aberdeen expresses. It was restored at Crewe Works coincidentally at the same time as privately-purchased No. 60007 *Sir Nigel Gresley*. While *Gresley* acquired garter blue livery, *Dominion of Canada* retained BR green.

It was shipped to Canada in April 1967. Also at the museum is LBSCR 'Terrier' 0-6-0T No. 54 *Waddon*, donated by British Railways in 1963 and exported on August 23, that year. Neither of the expatriate A4s nor *Waddon* have ever been steamed in preservation. ∎